ILLUSIONAL MARKETING

The Use of Storytelling, User Experience and Gamification in Business

Adnan Veysel ERTEMEL, PhD.

Zea Books
2021

ISBN 978-1-60962-189-6   print
ISBN 978-1-60962-190-2   ebook

doi 10.32873/unl.dc.zea.1275

Electronic (pdf) ebook edition available online at
https://digitalcommons.unl.edu/zeabook/

Print edition available from
http://www.lulu.com/spotlight/unllib

UNL does not discriminate based upon any protected status.
Please go to http://www.unl.edu/equity/notice-nondiscrimination

Nebraska
UNIVERSITY OF
Lincoln

To my dear family, who have never withheld their support...

We should all be concerned about the future because we will have to spend the rest of our lives there...

C. F. Kettering

ACKNOWLEDGMENTS

Writing this book would never have been possible without the courage and support of certain people...

Firstly, I would like to thank my esteemed Professor Aypar Uslu who has taught me the notion of marketing and brand and has always stood by me with her invaluable contributions to my academic career as a faculty member; and the Head of the Marketing Department at Marmara University, Professor Sahavet Gürdal who has guided me throughout my dissertation process and also later on as an academic with her valuable insights. I owe my valued teacher Professor Serdar Pirtini a debt of gratitude for providing me with his unconditional support since the very first years of my doctoral studies and has encouraged me to go onto the next level every time he invites me to the annual doctoral seminars at Marmara University since I started my career as a faculty member. I would also very much like to thank my esteemed teacher Professor Ali Rıza Kaylan from Boğaziçi University, for his ongoing support.

I would like to express my gratitude to Ercan Altuğ Yılmaz, gamification advisor, for his support in my writing of this book; to Michael Wu for offering a much-appreciated contribution to this book throughout our interviews that have brought new aspects of various kinds; to Sinan Sülün, storyteller, for his significant contributions on the subject of storytelling. Last but not least, I would like to thank İlhami Taş, the head of Kare Agency, for his worthwhile contributions in various aspects to my book through his precious ideas and to my Dear brother Sinan Ertemel who has always stood by me with his moral support.

PREFACE

We are going through such a period in which everything has become digitized, with the level of digitalization increasing progressively. On the one hand, numerous books on how to do marketing in a digital environment are being published; on the other hand, the books that explain decades-old marketing techniques time after time are still stacking the shelves pretending as if no such digitalization were actually taking place whatsoever... That being the case, at a time when digitalization is permeating every single aspect of life, there are not many studies that can actually go beyond the superficial descriptions of the digital revolution; that examine the new challenges brands are facing in the digital world; and that further explain the strategies required to engage new generation consumers. This book explores the new major challenges faced by brands and presents effective strategies in an entertaining fashion by providing interactive multimedia examples to the illusional marketing strategies that correspond with today's consumer.

In the light of examples based on the current marketing practices, this book explains which marketing strategies have completely lost their effectiveness and which strategies tend to align with and correspond to consumers. The content of the book is aimed to get a complete picture by synthesizing the existing strategies and adopting a holistic perspective.

Adnan Veysel ERTEMEL, PhD.

PREFACE FOR THE SECOND EDITION

This publication is a book upon which I have ventured to write with the encouragement of a couple of my esteemed scholar colleagues. Heartened by the positive feedback regarding the first edition, we organized a series of seminars under the name of "Illusional Techniques", working together as a team composed of experts who have brought unique contributions to the book's theoretical background based on their field of expertise, namely dear Sinan Sülün, storyteller and man of letters; dear Ercan Altuğ Yılmaz, gamification expert; and Mustafa Dalcı, the founder of Userspots, a visionary company in user experience. All of these names are experts in their respective fields. Accordingly, we have so far organized more than ten #illusionaltechniques summits mainly at universities in different cities. Illusional marketing is not a made-up concept; on the contrary, it is a conceptualization of the marketing techniques implemented by numerous brands in recent years drawing on behavioral psychology through an exploration with a holistic approach and the relevant theoretical background.

The term 'illusional' is quite thought-provoking indeed… However, an in-depth explanation as to why it is coined as such is later provided in the related section. Well, doesn't the concept of illusion also have negative connotations? Yes, but the part of the marketing practice that needs to be critiqued, that is, its ethical dimension, has become increasingly important and thus deserves the term 'illusion'. Illusional techniques are so powerful that they can save lives when used for good purposes, just like a sharp knife in the hands of a surgeon, so to speak. When used in malicious ways, however, they can make life miserable... For this very reason, we have started to discuss the other side of the story, namely "technology addiction as an architected phenomenon" in a series of seminars.

This book has been enriched in the light of your feedback with respect to its content. In addition, videos that may prove to be beneficial for the internalization of the concepts presented hereby are also included in the book. You can watch the videos at the end of the respective sections by scanning the quick response code (QR) with your phone.

I wish you a pleasant reading experience…

Adnan Veysel ERTEMEL, PhD.
Istanbul Commerce University,
Faculty of Business Administration
Istanbul, June 2020
adnan.ertemel@gmail.com

FOREWORD BY PROFESSOR PHILIP KOTLER

This book is a must-have for marketers who need to use a composite set of tools to break through the attention economy. The book is also for the general public who might be concerned about the growing and numbing screen time that takes people away from doing other things.

— Philip Kotler on Illusional Marketing

FOREWORD BY PROFESSOR SERDAR PİRTİNİ

We are going through a period in which not only technology is evolving rapidly but also consumer behavior is changing at a rapid pace. In such an environment, marketing concepts are inevitably transformed within new dimensions. Many strategies implemented previously in a successful way are now proven to be ineffective; and hence new approaches are being developed.

This book entitled *Illusional Marketing*, written by my dear student and esteemed colleague Adnan Veysel Ertemel, Ph.D. is one of the studies to be the first in its kind, complementing concepts such as neuromarketing in the field of marketing science.

Laying particular emphasis on behavioral psychology that has recently become prominent in the marketing science, *Illusional Marketing* explains the marketing practices in the new era as a guide to both the academic and business world through its contemporary examples… Therefore, I would like to congratulate Dr. Adnan Veysel Ertemel on his work, which is a major contribution to marketing science.

Prof. Serdar PİRTİNİ
Marmara University,
Faculty of Business Administration

FOREWORD BY MICHAEL WU

As a scientist, I always believe in data, causality relationships, meticulous analyses and verification. However, the decision-making process in humans is non-linear and not always rational. According to modern behavioral economists, we are '*Predictably Irrational*' beings...

In the competitive markets where there is a fierce competition to catch our limited attention, you have to address both the conscious and the subconscious brain. This book is an exclusive guide that offers you in-depth techniques that are beyond causality, analyses and verifications so as to appeal to the subconscious of consumers.

Michael WU, PhD.
Chief Scientist, Lithium Technologies

PROLOGUE

Digital revolution, gamification, storytelling and user experience design...

We have started to hear these concepts quite frequently in recent years. Accordingly, the reason for writing this book is due to the lack of a book in the market that examines the concepts mentioned above, which are often heard by business managers and marketing professionals who do not yet know how to handle them as a business strategy, with a strategic point of view and in the form that is spared from the technical elements...

When asked, professionals who practice user experience design and gamification techniques may not fully apprehend the big picture and know exactly what and why they are doing in the first place... Looking at the digital revolution from a broader perspective we can acknowledge that everything is changing in a stunning way, this book will aim at explaining the paradigm shift at a macro dimension and also revealing what is expected to remain stable and what will be changing in the upcoming century.

Accompanied by relevant examples with visual and video content, the book systematically analyzes the main reasons for many practices that are considered new implemented in the world of marketing and how they can be applied by looking from the perspective of business managers.

How do the QR (Quick Response) Codes Work?

In order to view the video examples mentioned throughout the book,

A smartphone or tablet with an internet connection is required.

Next, just install a QR code reader application on your device.

After typing "QR reader" on the search engine on the Internet, you may install and open one of the free programs.

When you open the program, the camera of your device will be activated.

Then, scan the QR code with your phone's camera.

It will automatically recognize the QR code.

After that, it is very simple to read any QR code you want!

Contents

INTRODUCTION

The 21st century is called the *information age*. Information technologies make up the infrastructure of this era and during the Internet revolution and aftermath, these technologies have gained impetus in this process. ***Let us bear in mind that we have not even completed the first quarter of the 21st century...***

Scenarios that used to be unimaginable previously now turn into reality one by one through the unprecedented developments in technology experienced in dimensions regarding ***accessing, storage, processing as well as interpretation*** of information. Such scenarios, being beyond technically viable, have indicated the processing of enormous volumes of data; and thanks to the exceptional advancements in information technologies, these scenarios can now be realized. This issue will be examined in detail in Part 1 of this book.

Marketing in a digital world has become more technical and measurable than ever before. Despite all the information that has been increasing, we all have 24 hours a day and our time does not increase even by one minute. In a world where the information produced is increasing exponentially, the active attention of consumers has become more and more scarce, and hence more valuable. Based on the fact that it is getting more and more difficult to attract the conscious attention of consumers, illusional marketing rests upon the idea of appealing to the unconscious.

Since the 1990s, particularly over the last two decades, psychologists have made important discoveries on how the human brain works and the basic underlying mechanics of human behaviors. The critical importance of the unconscious, known as the right brain, has been proven through new evidence for almost all the processes involved in, such as the moment a consumer comes across the brand for the first time, his / her interaction process and developing loyalty with the brand.

The fact that a psychologists, Daniel Kahnemann, won the 2002 Nobel Economy Prize with his mentioning of findings related to the unconscious in his book *Thinking, Fast and Slow*[1] pinpointed the increasing importance of behavioral economics. The importance of this issue is verified in a similar fashion with the development that the 2017 Nobel Prize was also won by a behavioral economics professor, Thaler, who based his book entitled *Nudge* (2016)[2] on the idea that consumers are not rational beings. The trend that started with psychology and went along with economics has continued to be influential in the marketing discipline as well over the recent years. Neuromarketing attempts to explain this phenomenon by examining the signals in the brain. Yet, such approaches remain to be in a tactical dimension.

This book studies the effect of the unconscious upon marketing on a different level. The book makes a conceptualization under the name of illusional marketing by examining storytelling, gamification and user experience design techniques that draw on different disciplines which have frequently been resorted to over the recent years, and all of which are directed towards the unconscious through the lenses of marketing.

> *In an information-oriented world where everything has become digitalized, ironically, brands are making use of behavioral psychology by addressing the subconscious as a sole remedy to engage consumers.*

The first step a brand should consider in illusional marketing is that it should consider creating a brand story that resonates with its consumers. Afterwards, user experience design is the second step that rests upon the principle that consumers use the products intuitively without exerting

---

[1] Daniel Kahneman, *Thinking, Fast and Slow*, Farrar, Straus and Giroux, 2011.
[2] Richard H. Thaler & Cass R. Sunstein, *Nudge: Improving Decisions About Health, Wealth, and Happiness*, Yale University Press, 2008.

much effort, which is enabled through addressing the subconscious as an alternative and more concrete method in an environment in which it has become more difficult to attract the active and conscious attention of consumers. The single motto of user experience design is "don't make me think". That is, guide the users in their journey in such a way that they don't have to spend any conscious mental effort. This design is made based on the users' unconscious behaviors in similar relevant processes. Ultimately, by lowering the cost that is borne in the value formula in marketing, the maximization of the perceived value is ensured.

Last but not least, gamification aims at increasing consumers' motivation to engage with the brands in the desired way. In gamification, the elements of a game such as competition, leader boards, scores and badges are added into the product and service use process. Thus, consumers become players and the use of the products is rendered more enjoyable.

Even though the efficiency of such techniques has been proven, it is not always possible to achieve success immediately when you say "Let's now gamify our processes or why don't we employ storytelling?" This book provides a step by step explanation as to what needs to be done so that these techniques can be implemented correctly along with the related success stories.

References

1. Kahneman, Daniel. *Thinking, Fast and Slow*. New York: Farrar, Straus and Giroux, 2011.

2. Thaler, Richard H., & Sunstein, Cass R. *Nudge: Improving Decisions About Health, Wealth, and Happiness.* New Haven: Yale University Press, 2008.

PART 1

THE BIG PICTURE IN THE DIGITAL REVOLUTION

Philosophy of Knowledge at the Dawn of the Information Age

It is impossible for us to see the big picture without examining the basic characteristics of the current century, namely the information age, we are living in. Now, let us have a look at information from a different perspective and explore the power of digitalization.

"Everything has a dimension related to matter and to knowledge" is the most fundamental model philosophers have used throughout history to describe the universe and phenomena. The most basic assumption that continued to be accepted to be true, starting from the history of humanity up until a very recent period, was that the matter was infinite, while knowledge was finite. Yet, in the recent period, it has been understood that the matter, namely the sources in nature such as water and energy, is not infinite. On the other hand, it has been revealed that knowledge is not finite; on the contrary, as explained in this part, production of knowledge on an infinite dimension as well as access to knowledge is possible. Accordingly, this shift in the very basic assumption has led the center of gravity to shift from the dimension of the matter over to that of the knowledge. This shift also requires a change in the mindset regarding knowledge.

Knowledge and the Changing Mindset

If we examine the mindset that has been at stake to access knowledge from the past till the present day, we see that communication in the form of one-dimensional monologue has been fundamentally changed., Contrary to one dimensional nature of access to information in the form of books, newspapers, radio and television, the Internet has brought about two-way communication with consumers. [3]

At present, it is possible for a brand to track the frequency of consumers that search a particular range of product in a particular geographical area as well as the seasonal change in their purchase habits by means of Google Trends. By using this kind of data, airline companies can mark up their ticket prices in real-time by monitoring the change in the search volume in Google Trends since they can check, in real-time, the volume of those planning to fly to a certain city within a definite period just after an international sports derby draw. In fact, measurability is the biggest weapon of digital media.

As can be understood from the examples provided above, this feature of the Internet conveys a drastic change in the interaction with information even if it is not that evident from the very beginning. This paradigm shift is also the strongest weapon of digitalization. Based on this, it is essential to progress by measuring the return of each and every step that has been taken in the eye of the consumers. We will examine these weapons in detail in Part 1 - the New Weapons of Brands.

Advances in Information Technologies

Now let us have a closer look at the unprecedented developments that occur in *accessing, storing, processing* and *interpreting* of data technologies as mentioned in the introduction part.

1. Data Storage Technologies

The cost of storing data is now declining to a negligible dimension. Any Facebook user, among billions of them, can now click the 'live' button any time and shoot a video in HD quality. These videos are constantly saved too. Facebook is able to offer this service to all of its users permanently and free of charge. In addition to the information produced on the conventional Internet and social media, smart objects in daily life such as automobiles, thermostats and refrigerators will be able to produce data constantly 7/24 through the growing Internet of Things (IoT). It is predicted that by

---

[3] Rick Levine, *Cluetrain Manifesto,* Basic Books, 2009.

the mid 2020s, the number of sessions opened by smart objects on the internet will be 60 times more than those opened by human beings. The cost of storing data that has a massive amount, named as big data, that would not be possible to be managed through conventional data management techniques has been declining significantly over the years.

In addition to the data storage cost, data processing cost has also been showing a dramatic downward trend.

Besides all these developments, brand-new data storage technologies have been developed that accelerate this trend. One such recent development is that 700 terabytes of data can be saved onto a single (1) gram of DNA through the technology that utilizes DNA spirals for data storage.[4] The DNA spiral is so tiny that data open to everyone in the world can be fit into a size of a shoebox by means of this technology. Some of the major technology companies are planning to transport all their data centers onto the DNA technology, accordingly.[5]

2. Access to Information: Cloud Computing and Marketing Automation

All sorts of content applications and platforms have been transformed into cloud-based systems across the globe, which enables the diverse service providers and applications to work with one another in an integrated fashion through the Application Programming Interfaces (APIs), with access to anything being just a click away. Advanced analytics services, CRM solutions, email services, service desk operations and much more functionality can be used in combination with cloud as the common denominator. Coupled together, these services can significantly increase value add provided to brands and ultimately to consumers.

---

[4] Sebastian Anthony, "Harvard cracks DNA storage, crams 700 terabytes of data into a single gram," *Extreme Tech,* updated 17 August 2012. http://www.extremetech.com/extreme/134672-harvard-cracks-dna-storage-crams-700-terabytes-of-data-into-a-single-gram

[5] John Markman, "DNA Is The New Data Storage" *Forbes,* 22 July 2016 http://www.forbes.com/sites/jonmarkman/2016/07/22/dna-is-the-new-data-storage/2/#26b0449e15fb

3. Interpreting Information and Artificial Intelligence

According to Moore's law, the processor speed doubles every 20 months. The exponential increase in information processing and the dramatic decrease in its cost have led to a breakthrough in artificial intelligence technology.

Artificial intelligence technologies are advancing in such a way that they are capable of enabling solutions in the form of a personal assistant by observing all the actions of those around them in the long-run, and thereby 'learn', as it is in the case of newborn baby's learning process. Apple's Siri, Microsoft's Cartona and Amazon's Alexa are some of the examples of artificial intelligence technologies that receive a significant amount of investment, and yet are still very much in their infancy.

To illustrate this point, we may provide the example of Apple's Siri which was not able to comprehend many questions of its users or respond correctly either in its very first version. Now, Siri is capable of producing wittier jokes. It is predicted that it could be possible to have real time translation and / or interpreting services from and to all languages spoken across the globe, including those with accents, easily in the near.

In the future, smart personal assistants will be able to make a recommendation to you about how you may respond to an email by analyzing diverse information such as the personal life of the individuals, their correspondences, preferences and so many other related elements. In addition, it is foreseen that these assistants will be so sensitive and smart that they could even make decisions on what time you would have to leave a business meeting by having a glance at massive data such as the participants, items on the agenda and the course of the meeting in a professional setting.

Another example we can give is from popular media. The movie *Her*, with its futuristic outlook towards artificial intelligence, successfully addresses the potential developments that the world may encounter.

Systems that can understand the individual, his / her life preferences and state of mind to an extent that is claimed can be considered highly futuristic by some. The following could be an answer to those who uphold such an opinion: excitement, enthusiasm, critical tone and other similar sentiments can be detected through the analysis of whatever an individual shares on social media by means of the sentiment analysis technique. Accordingly, thanks to advancing technology, specialized systems are being developed which can track the characteristics of the shared elements in the long-term, detect the state of mind of an individual, identify if the person has been in love over the last months as well as make recommendations whether the person needs a holiday at a particular point of time.

Figure 1.1: A fragment from the futuristic love movie *Her* depicting the first artificial intelligence operating system (Video)

In today's highly digitized world, marketing has become more technical and measurable than ever before...

4. Data Analysis with Big Data

Brands can now gain considerable insight regarding their customers through big data; and this insight is not a sort that has been explored before. By means of big data analysis over hundreds of thousands of social media shares, brands are able to detect their position in the eye of their customers vis-a-vis their competitors at a level the brand itself is not even aware of. In this way, brands can determine what requires to be produced next.

Data is the New Oil

Interpreting big data to produce value add is the most important task of this century. "Brand association maps" can be given as an example which can help brands gain customer insight by analyzing millions of social media posts. These maps include very important clues for brands. For example, Figure 1.2 presents the brand association map which has been obtained from an analysis that is based on hundreds of thousands of social media shares with regard to the Nike brand.

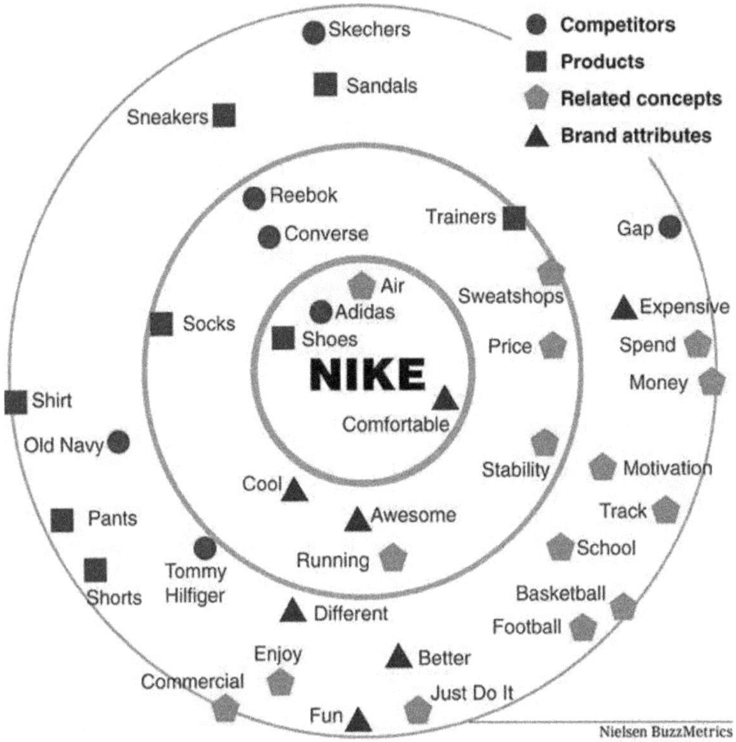

Figure 1.2: Nike Brand Association Map-Nielsen Buzz Metrics[6]

[6] Nielsen "BuzzMetrics Brand Associate Map," accessed 23 Sept 2016.
http://www.nielsen.com/content/dam/nielsen/en_us/docu-
ments/pdf/Fact%20Sheets/Nielsen%20Brand%20Association%20Map%20-
%20US.pdf

Using techniques like sentiment analysis, the sentiment in expressions contained in consumers' social media posts are analyzed to understand how they feel about the brand in relation to competitors etc. Such techniques are very helpful to gather great insights as they collectively represent how the society feels and thinks about a brand as a whole. In brands association maps, you can, for instance, understand what comes (as product category, brand attributes, related concept) to consumers' mind first when the brand is mentioned. Note that the more a related term is to the center of the map, the more prominent it is with regard to the brand.

Shift from Papyrus to Paper, Super Computers to IoT

> *We are all part of the change; you either manage change or are defeated by it...*

Back in the old ages, many people used to come together to be able to write a book on the papyruses. Following the invention of the printing press in the 1400s, the writing of books became easier in time. Gradually, the cost of paper declined quickly. Thus, it became easier to own paper and indirectly to own a book. While it was impossible even to conceive that one would have a personal library in his / her house previously, this became possible in the early 1900s, despite being a bit costly. In our day, the cost of paper is at such a negligible level that we use it and then dispose of it.

Let us now make the same analogy for computers. Computers have also undergone a kind of evolution that is very similar to that of paper.

In the 1950s, a computer took up a vast space as big as a room, and a lot of people used to connect to one single supercomputer. After years, the notion of *personal computers (PCs)*, which was inconceivable in the earlier times, became a reality in the 1980s. Today, computer, microchip and sensor technologies are growing at a fast pace, while their costs are declining quickly to negligible dimensions. In the vision of the Internet of Things, almost all objects can turn into a smart object through the microchips embedded in the object that allows viability for doing so, like in the example of disposable paper. By the same rationale, the costs have reached a negligible level in the data storage area as well.

These revolutionary changes in computer and microchip technology will lead to new dramatic changes in the mindset of humankind as we have touched upon in the part entitled Philosophy of Knowledge. We may provide an example related to a world in which almost everything is smart and can be saved, and no concern exists whatsoever regarding the data storage capacity: it became compulsory in Russia to install a front and rear camera in the vehicle to be used in cases of accidents; and this was made compulsory for all the vehicles. In the event of an accident, the vehicle senses the impact through its sensors and detects that an accident has occurred, thus, it does not delete the last few minutes of the record imagery of the accident, and rather it sends the recording to a central provider via the Internet. Now, let us imagine that the same rationale is implemented on a product that is similar to Google Glass. For the parents, their baby's first utterance of words that make sense must be very special. We all have such memories in our lives we wish we could have had the chance to save the moment and have a video of it. Wouldn't it be great if a constant recording technology were available that could record an image of a special memory you wish to save even if time had elapsed by your utterance of the command "Hey Google! Record what I have just seen as a video." There is no reason why this cannot be realized in the world of the Internet of Things in which no concern exists whatsoever with regard to storage, cost or dimension.

Similarly, companies were not used to store all the data related to their customers in the past due to this being not feasible owing to the data storage costs. Now, they can do it for all of their customers, not only for VIP customers per se; but also for all sorts of data types that one may imagine. What's more, they can make use of the other data that could be significant for a particular customer and that is somewhere on the Internet apart from the data kept by the companies themselves for their customers.

The New Normal: Digital is Completely Integrated into Daily Life

The 21st century, in other words the information age, is heading towards a path that will be an integral part of our lives. So, what is the world in which digital is the "new normal" going to be like? A new technology attracts the attention of the consumers to the extent that it is successful. Rare technologies that have managed to become part of life literally become embedded in the background. In this phenomenon that is named 'ubiquity', technology at stake is in fact everywhere and it is embedded in the background of life so well that at the same time it is not anywhere though, in other words, it is not even noticed or conspicuous. The best example of this is actually electricity which is everywhere in our lives, but we do not notice its existence. Another relevant example is the railways. The graph provided below presents the frequency of the word 'railways' in all the books that have been written in the world. The search is done via Google Books as an objective criterion of how a particular technology has been taken for granted and accepted to be normal by the society over the years. As a very popular concept in the 1920s, this technology has started to be mentioned less in books written, which reveals that this technology, as a part of life, has been taken for granted in time.

When Technology Becomes Completely Adapted, it Becomes Invisible! Frequency of 'Railways' in Books

Frequency of 'Railways' in Google Books

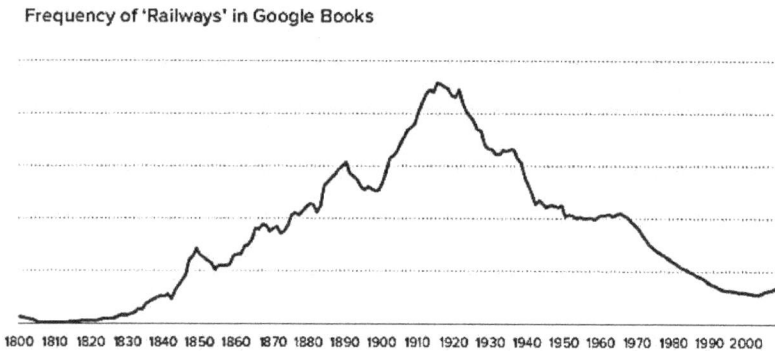

1800 1810 1820 1830 1840 1850 1860 1870 1880 1890 1900 1910 1920 1930 1940 1950 1960 1970 1980 1990 2000

Figure 1.3: The frequency of the word 'Railways' in all the books.[7]

---

[7] *Google Books* . Accessed Date 23.09.2016. https://books.google.com.tr/.

Likewise, when we do a search for the word 'software', we see that this word reached a peak in terms of popularity in books in the 2000s, and then it has started to show a downward trend afterwards.

When Technology Becomes Completely Adapted, it Becomes Invisible! Frequency of 'Software' in Books

Frequency of 'Software' in Google Books

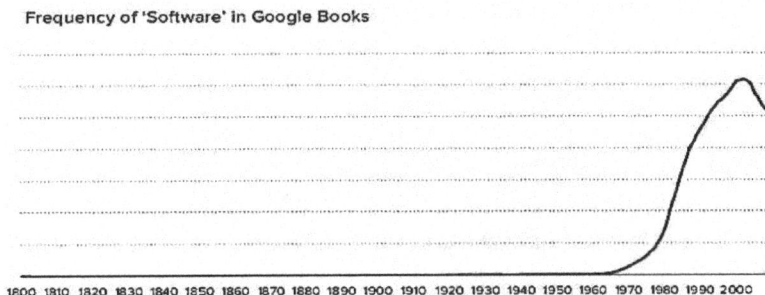

1800 1810 1820 1830 1840 1850 1860 1870 1880 1890 1900 1910 1920 1930 1940 1950 1960 1970 1980 1990 2000

Figure 1.6: The frequency of the word 'Software' in all the books published

The Potential of Big Data: A Blogger's Struggle with Amazon

Now, let us examine a scenario that would shed light on the real potential of big data. Imagine that you are a blogger who has tens of thousands of followers. You order a tablet computer from Amazon website. Yet, the order was   delivered at a much later date than what had been promised. What's more, you realize that the tablet is broken when you try to turn it on. With the impact of this bad user experience you have been through, you write a rather negative review about Amazon on your blog. Imagine that the call center of the company calls you on the very same day. The customer representative says that they have examined the file and they will send a tablet to you free of charge in order to make amends for the inconvenience caused. Everything is typical up until this point. The   interesting part of the story starts from this point on. The customer representative asks you an utterly extraordinary question:

"Sir, as far as we have seen, you want your orders to be delivered to your office address. Yet, what is seen from your Linkedin profile is that you started to work for a new company as of last week. We congratulate you

29

on your new job! As far as we have observed from your check-ins on Four-square, you are on vacation now. We wish you a great holiday! Which address would you like us to deliver your order?"

Yes, Amazon customer representative says all these! In today's world in which the cost of data storage and data processing has been reduced down to a negligible level, proactive brands no longer suffice with the data they already have within themselves. They would rather collect very diverse data clusters related to their customers from the media on the Internet open to everyone, thus, they can gain 360° insight. Moreover, they can do this not only for their most valuable customers but for all of their customers. As it is in the case of Amazon.com scenario, do not think that data access is illicit or illegal. Within the terms and conditions you accept in the sign up processes of new generation companies such as LinkedIn and Foursquare, there exists the condition of sharing data with third parties!

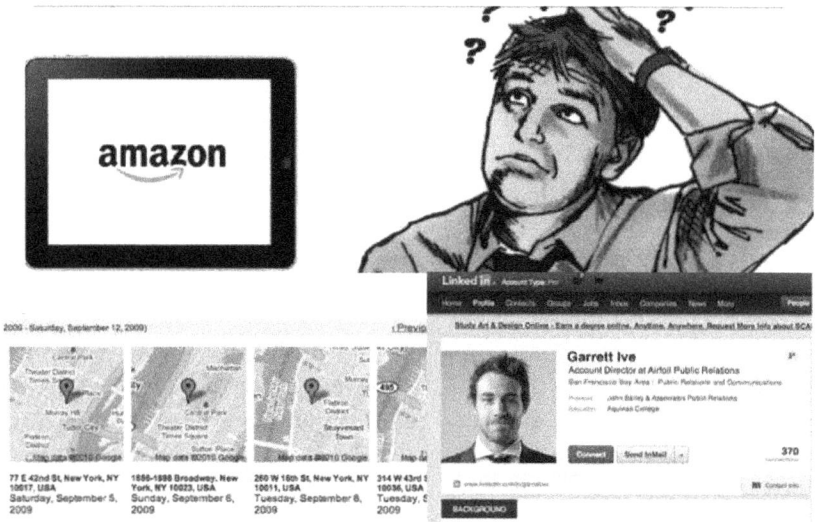

Figure 1.5 Customer Insight with Big Data– Amazon.com Example

Algorithmic Marketing

In almost every aspect of our lives in our current day, we increasingly encounter customized services personalized completely on an individual basis through programming with algorithms. The results of the search we make via the Google search render customization possible based on who we are, as well as our browsing and clicking history. Likewise, the newsfeed we see on social media is also presented before us after having been customized by algorithms. The claim that Russians had interfered and engaged in manipulations over social media for the 2016 US elections, which Trump won, remained on the agenda for quite a long time. Putting the Facebook company in a very difficult position, Cambridge Analytica scandal was the most evident proof that it was possible to retrieve personalized elements and launch campaigns intended for a particular individual by making use of big data and analyzing who the media consumers are, their friends as well as their likes on social media.

Industry 4.0 and Society 5.0

The notion of Industry 4.0 refers to the use of robotics and autonomous systems in every step of the production process. The notion of Society 5.0, as put forth by Japan, rests upon the use of big data by interpreting it so as to build the super smart cities of the future. In that regard, its scope is not limited to the use of artificial intelligence and robotic systems only in industrial production. Unlike Industry 4.0, Society 5.0 is guided by a vision of robotic systems that work in a humane way, learning in a *human centric* fashion and starting to have feelings in time. A good example of this can be found in the excerpt in which the movie *Her*. It is foreseen that technological and social interaction of human beings will change drastically as a result of the sensors and smart devices that could be found everywhere in the smart cities of the future. In short, a fusion of virtual world and physical world is intended and targeted by Society 5.0.

Software is Eating the World

One of the earliest entrepreneurs of Silicon Valley, Marc Andreessen, the founder of the first internet browser Mosaic and Netscape has been investing in technology companies for many years. In one of his renowned papers, he maintained that software companies are going to overtake almost all the sectors in the world within a decade.[8]

According to Andreessen, the driving forces of this related process are as follows:

☐ Due to owning a mobile smart phone (penetration), consequently the rate of access to the Internet, occupies a significant portion of the world population.

☐ Access to knowledge and education contents has become easier thanks to the Internet, which enables methods regarding entrepreneurship like lean start-ups to expand quickly. Thus, potential entrepreneurs can emerge not only from Silicon Valley but also from even a remote part of the world.

☐ Since digital products are consumed in the virtual environment, they can expand cross borders easily; hence, they can acquire customers across the globe. Most importantly, the potential customer market that can purchase the products amounts approximately to 2 billion.

Digitalization is in the position of being the most fundamental dynamic of transformation in almost all industries. Even sectors that were thought to have no relation with the digital world in the recent past, namely agriculture, construction and medicine, have gone through digital transformation through which their business models are being rewritten. This transformation occurs on three different planes, which are:

---

[8] Marc Andreessen, "Why Software Is Eating The World," *Wall Street Journal*, 20 August 2011; https://www.wsj.com/articles/SB10001424053111903480904576512250915629460

- Industries that did not have any relation with software in the past are reinforced and enriched through software. Such industries are software-supported lighting systems, defense industry, automobiles and television.
- Having been affected by the digital revolution in a disruptive way, sectors whose models of business doing and income have been written entirely once again. Examples of such sectors are music and entertainment.
- Born-digital platforms such as Google, Amazon, YouTube and Facebook.

Table 1: Disruptive Effect of Software on Other Industries

	Dimension	Examples of Industries
1	Industries that had no connection with software in the past has become stronger through software	Automobile, Aircraft, Lighting Industry
2	Industries whose business models have been disruptively affected by software and written once again	Music, Movie Industries, Media Industry, (soon transportation and hotel industries)
3	New digital platforms that are completely based on software	Google, YouTube, Facebook, Amazon, Skype

The New Leaders of the Transformation

The new analytic technologies in the digital toolbox engages in "Growth Hacking" so as to reach the ideal customers through the most appropriate recommendation and sales model, which renders the optimization of business models possible. It is possible to obtain relevant information to understand what customers are thinking by instant digital public opinion polls via social media management tools instead of resorting to methods like conventional one-to-one meetings and surveys that last for many months.

The new toolbox used by brands while making strategic decisions has started to be mainly composed of digital tools. Until the recent past, there used to be only the CIO (Chief Information Officer) position in the corporations, and this position represents the digital world at the same level and status with the general manager and deputy general manager. However, this status refers to a supplementary mission rather than the primary functions of the corporation. In fact, the need for executive managers who can develop business strategy and digital strategy in marketing has arisen with the advent of digitalization. For this reason, today, new leaders who both come from the digital world and also have a good command of marketing are strongly needed. The new defined position for such leaders who are the future CEO candidates is *Chief Digital Officer (CDO)*.

References

3. Levine, Rick. *Cluetrain Manifesto*. New York: Basic Books, 2009.

4. Anthony, Sebastian. "Harvard cracks DNA storage, crams 700 terabytes of data into a single gram," *Extreme Tech*, updated 17 August 2012.

   http://www.extremetech.com/extreme/134672-harvard-cracks-dna-storage-crams-700-terabytes-of-data-into-a-single-gram

5. Markman, John. "DNA Is the New Data Storage," *Forbes,* 22 July 2016 http://www.forbes.com/sites/jonmarkman/2016/07/22/dna-is-the-new-data-storage/2/#26b0449e15fb

6. Nielsen. "BuzzMetrics Brand Associate Map" http://www.nielsen.com/content/dam/nielsen/en_us/documents/pdf/Fact%20Sheets/Nielsen%20Brand%20Association%20Map%20-%20US.pdf accessed 9 Sept 2016.

7. *Google Books* https://books.google.com.tr/ accessed 9 Sept 2016.

8. Andreessen, Marc. "Why Software Is Eating the World." *Wall Street Journal*, 20 August 2011. https://www.wsj.com/articles/SB10001424053111903480904576512250915629460

PART 2

NEW PROBLEMS AND NEW WEAPONS OF BRANDS

The New Problems of Brands

The challenges faced by the brands are much different than those two decades ago. Those challenges are discussed in the remainder of this chapter.

Globalization and Increased Competition

Growing globalization and supply surplus lead to an increasingly competitive environment all around the world. The advertising budget, which brands spend in order to attract consumers in the midst of increasing competition, has increased considerably. Therefore, there is a significant rise in the number of brand-related messages.

The Social Media Revolution and the New Language of Communication

Social media has literally brought about a revolution in communication. Consumers have lost their trust in brands in an inverse proportion to the budget that brands spend on advertising. So what resources do consumers resort to when making a decision? The answer to this is simple. With the advent of the social media revolution, consumers have started to pay attention to the feedback and recommendations of other consumers (peer-to-peer - P2P) who are in the same position with them and regard such feedback as the most reliable source. Besides taking into account the recommendations from their acquaintances, consumers also consider the suggestions from people they do not know. In a study conducted by Nielsen, the ratio of relying on reviews and recommendations on social media is 70%, while the rate of trust in recommendations from acquaintances is around 92%.[9] Consumers tend to receive advice from other consumers who are in the same position as themselves. The trust for reviews and recommendations on social media is around 70% and for friends' recommendations, this rate is around 90%. Hence, one-to-one verbal communication has become an increasingly significant strategy.

Social media has now turned the passive knowledge consumers of the past into active information producers. When the volume of information produced on the Internet is examined, 2008 is considered to be a turning point. It is seen that the majority of the information produced in 2008 and onwards has been, in effect, the information produced on social media by consumers. Brands are left with no other option than trying to become a part of the chats between the consumers. In the past, brands that used to look down on consumers used to be highly in demand, giving the impression that they were flawless. And yet, the Internet and social media have triggered revolutionary changes in communication. Transparency, sincerity and being humanistic have become the key concepts of the new era.

The genetic codes of this new era were first articulated in 1999 in *The Cluetrain Manifesto*, which was written by a group of visionary opinion leaders. *The Cluetrain Manifesto* states that the Internet is misinterpreted by brands, and is solely seen as a new means for their sales channels. In fact, the Internet has triggered a highly serious revolution[3]. An extensive virtual environment full of discussions and chats has just emerged among people and this chat environment is moving at the speed of light, which has allowed people to exchange information about brands much more quickly than the brands themselves. *The Cluetrain Manifesto* starkly revealed the paradigm shift experienced owing to the Internet revolution. Indeed, brands have had to accept the fact that they are on equal footing with the consumers; therefore, they are supposed to adopt a humane attitude by listening instead of talking so that they could become a part of the ongoing discussions on social media. This new communication language

---

[9] Nielsen "Trust Barometer Report," accessed 23 Sept 2016. http://www.nielsen.com/us/en/insights/reports-downloads/2012/global-trust-in-advertising-and-brand-messages.html

manifests itself even in brand logos. The message conveyed by using capital letters in social media conversations often refers to a high-pitched speech to suppress and outdo the opposite side. Accordingly, the use of capital letters in brand logos reflected the supercilious style of the brands. In parallel with the revolution in the communication language and this new understanding, we observe that all letters, including the initial ones, are now written in lowercase in logos as well.

The exponential increase in the volume of information produced by both brands and social media leads to the attention economy, also known as the paradox of plenty. This seems to be the biggest challenge for brands in the coming years. Now let us examine the attention economy in detail.

The New Challenge and Attention Economy

In the 1980s, IT managers promised that "We would soon have information at our fingertips". Yes, in today's world in which smartphones have entered our lives, information is now at our fingertips. However, in the midst of all the things that require to be paid attention to, unless extra attention is paid to read the information that is at the tip of our fingers, no one will ever be aware of such information...

Statistics show that the lifespan of a 'tweet that has escaped our notice and has not been retweeted' is 2 hours at most, and the 'this tweet' gets lost in the ocean of information. Nowadays, the bandwidth in communication networks is no longer regarded as an issue, yet it is the bandwidth of human beings with regard to their processing of information which has become critical...

Figure 2.2 Information at the tip of our fingers

The leading reason for the exponential increase in the volume of information produced is the social media revolution. Now every consumer also has the role of being an information producer at the same time. YouTube, Twitter and Instagram are some examples of platforms based on user generated content (UGC). A greater amount of information will be produced in the Internet of Things world, which expresses the intermachine communication. In the early 2020s, the number of sessions to be opened on our behalf by smart machines is expected to be much higher than the number of sessions we open ourselves. In such an era, the allotted time we have to devote to all of this work is just 24 hours and it is not possible to increase this time even by a single minute.

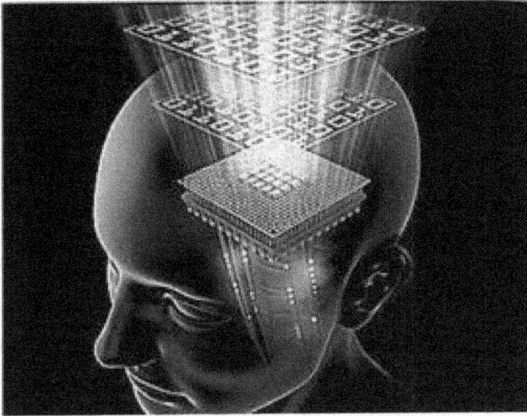

Figure 2.3: The New Bottleneck of the New World:
Our Speed of Perception

Herbert Simon, who first introduced the concept of the attention economy, stated that rapid increase in information caused poverty of attention.[10]

Wealth of information = Poverty of attention

"A wealth of information creates a poverty of attention."

-- Herbert Simon

All we have is 24 hours and despite the increase in information, it is not possible to increase this time even by a single minute.

---

[10] Herbert A. Simon, "Designing Organizations for an Information-Rich World," in *Computers, Communications, and the Public Interest,* Johns Hopkins University Press, 1971.

Attention can be described as the "**focused mental engagement**" that occurs between awareness and decision-making steps with regard to any phenomenon. In other words, attention is the missing link that acts as a unifier in the decision-making process.

We become aware of the issues at hand, and after an unconscious phase of reduction, we pay attention to some of them, and then we decide whether to take action or not.[11]

We can construe the concept of attention, in its fullest sense, as the most valid asset of the information age. The simplest example is that some businesses abroad offer consumers a free DVD player provided that they watch a certain number of advertisements. Currently, it is estimated that ¼ of the operating expenses in the US is intended simply to persuade consumers. And this rate is constantly on the rise.

On the other hand, consumers no longer read more than the first few sentences of an article they encounter. For this very reason, solutions that present the reader the gist of the subject and even challenge the information producer by saying "Express yourself in 140 characters", like Twitter, have come to the fore.

Similarly, the first 5 to 8 seconds of the video being watched is of critical importance. The content that is not found to be interesting enough is immediately closed and the next video is switched to. The new ad structure of YouTube, in which the video can only be skipped in the first 5 seconds simply by clicking the "Skip" button if that video is not liked, seems to make good use of this phenomenon in a very clever fashion. In addition, it is possible to see the impact of the attention economy in the movie and media industry as well. The first 20-30 seconds of TV series and trailers of the new films that come out are prepared with particular attention in an effort to make them as appealing as possible.

---

[11] Thomas H. Davenport & John C. Beck, *The Attention Economy: Understanding the New Currency of Business,* Harvard Business School Press, 2001.

> *It's harder than ever to convince the consumers to interact by attracting their attention...*

Attention Economy

As is the case with every marketing process, there is a **value exchange** in the attention economy as well. Yet, the exchange process in the attention economy is indirect. There is an invisible trust-based contract between consumers and service providers. Accordingly, consumers give their limited and valuable attention as well as their time to the service provider; in return, they receive services that are relevant, personalized and useful, and thus sticky in time. This situation continues as long as the promised services continue to be provided under the same conditions. Service providers that are able to attract the attention of the consumers for a certain period of time turn this attention into money easily and in an indirect way.

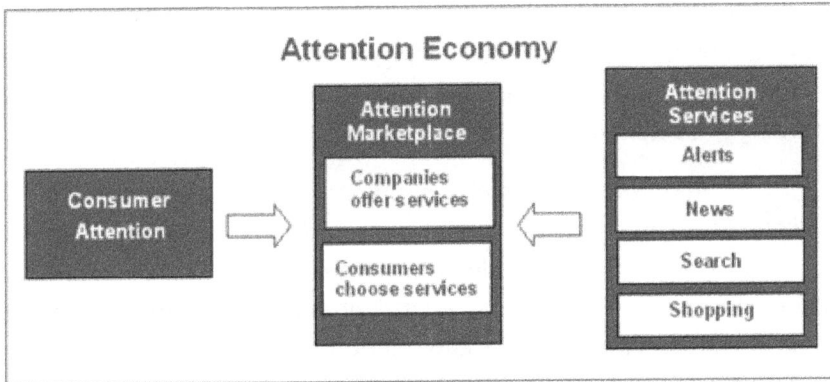

Figure 2.5: Structure of the Attention Economy

As a good example of this, Twitter has managed to become one of the most popular companies in Silicon Valley for it has successfully managed to attract the attention of consumers despite the fact that since its establishment it has not had a model of income for many years.

Providing relevant and personalized services, the service provider can better understand consumers on a one-on-one basis and render the service to the consumer in a more personalized manner in line with increasingly relevant results. This situation continues in the form of a loop that is strengthened over time and the service provider becomes indispensable over time gaining a great competitive advantage. An important element here is that interaction is not limited to direct interaction so as to understand consumers on a one-to-one scale. The consumer's surfing and clicking behavior also reveals key clues about the preferences of that person.

Amazon.com offers a list of recommendations headlined with "customers who bought this item also bought" by analyzing the customers' browsing history and what books they have reviewed.

Google is another successful company that recognizes the value of the consumers' limited time and attention. Completely isolated from banners and similar ads that could distract attention, it presents a simple experience by showing the most 'relevant' results on the search engine. With this structure, Google effortlessly distinguished itself from its competitors like Yahoo and AltaVista in the early 2000s, and in time, it has succeeded in turning this attention into money in an indirect way.

The importance and impact of the attention economy is also felt in emails and call center solutions. While junk (spam) e-mails used to be seen as a serious headache that would kill the time and attention of online consumers, they are no longer regarded as a problem thanks to the developments in spam filtering software and solutions that facilitate the e-mail experience such as Gmail. When the evolution of call centers is examined, the call centers that used to keep consumers on the phone for minutes on end have eventually been replaced by solutions that transfer customers to the related unit by dialing the necessary number based on the matter along with some recent further solutions that enable customers to voice their wishes. The use of Siri-style solutions on smartphones is also becoming increasingly more widespread.

In short, in our age, in which goods and services have become the same, and in which there is an explosion of exponential information that is far beyond an abundant level of knowledge, the prosperous enterprises of tomorrow will not be the ones that are able to produce more information, but rather the ones that not only catch and maintain the consumers' attention but also help manage their attention more efficiently in the face of an ever growing number of options.

Changing Marketing Orientations

In this section, the evolution of the marketing discipline as well as the current situation will be examined along with its background.

The Evolution of Consumers

Human beings have been evolving into being more and more complicated creatures as they get immune to various tactics over time, hence, it becomes harder to persuade, influence and amaze them. In the early years of the history of cinema, a horror film used to be the product of a much more primitive work. In the early days of the silver screen, the 50-second-long film called *The Arrival of a Train*, the first horror film in history, was nothing more than a train image that approached a station and people getting on and off the train in complete disarray. However, it is stated that some of the newly acquired audiences of the era who had not yet been acquainted with movies escaped from the movie hall with fear.

Arrival of a Train at La Ciotat (The Lumière Brothers, 1895) - YouTube

Figure 2.10: The First Horror Film in History (!): *The Arrival of a Train*

https://youtu.be/pT1zKlvOcxq

And yet in today's world, horror films are still not terrifying enough to be able to scare the audience. This situation, as in the film *Paranormal Activity*, in a way, pushes the film producers to use unusual new techniques to frighten the viewers...

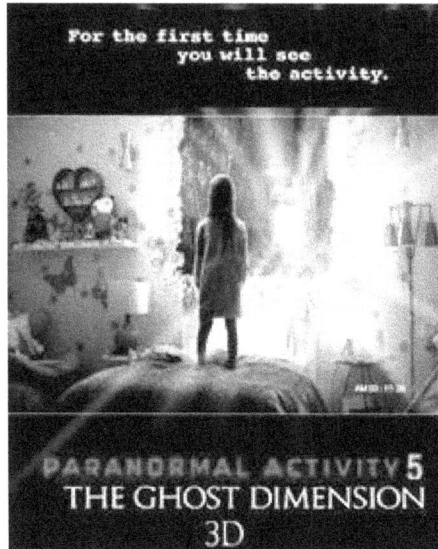

Figure 2.11: When ordinary tactics do not work to frighten the viewers: *Paranormal Activity*

https://youtu.be/X3eWIhXyBNo

Starbucks Roastery App Experience

The first movie of the History 1896

Paranormal Activity

Some examples are behind this QR Code:

https://www.youtube.com/playlist?list=PLC069zaQCEuBMnUT3IqQLPwTu1UkCjHEf

What Do Consumers Really Want?

Everything that is new becomes normal after a while. Consumers take new things for granted very quickly and always demand more from brands. Consumers want things that no other competitor has, things that only your brand can offer and will make them feel better. The keyword here is to make the consumer feel better. When the products sold in the past were no longer sufficient, complementary services were added into the process to differentiate in competition and to make customers feel better. For today's customers, however, complementary services are no longer found satisfactory. It has become required to design and offer an entirely authentic experience to the customers.

Experiential Marketing

Experiential marketing is based on the fact that consumers are not just rational beings who just make a purchase decision but they are also beings with emotions and feelings.[12] Experiential marketing and experience economy were first introduced by Alvin Toffler (1970).[13] Based on the idea that human beings are emotional creatures, experiential marketing aims to create positive associations about a brand and its products by appealing to their senses of sight, hearing, touch, taste, and smell as much as possible; thus, creating authentic experiences. For brand differentiation, it is critical that the brand create a truly authentic and unforgettable experience rather than just making do with the product and its supplementary services.

---

[12] Bernd Schmitt, "Experiential Marketing," *Journal of Marketing Management*, vol. 15, no. 1-3 (Apr. 1999), pp. 53-67.
[13] Alvin Toffler, *Future Shock*, Random House, 1970.

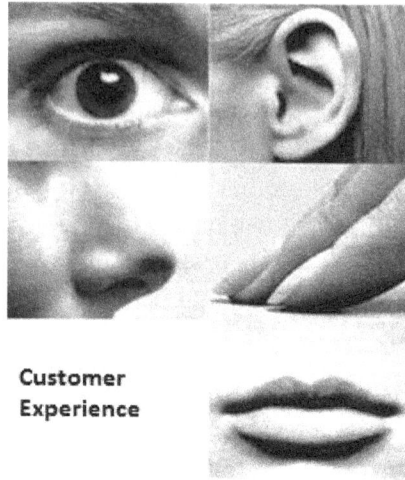

Customer
Experience

Figure 2.6: Customer Experience: Addressing all the Five Sense
Organs in Experiential Marketing

The Evolution of Marketing: From Products to Services and From Services to Experiences

In the past, it sufficed to market products via the right channel and promotion, acting in accordance with the dimensions of the marketing, namely, product, price, place and promotion (the 4 Ps of marketing), called the marketing mix. As can be seen obviously in the automobile sector, enriching the products with complementary services in time has become a sine qua non for differentiation. And yet, even complementary services are not enough to ensure differentiation today. Issues such as how the brand is at the forefront, what kind of an end-to-end experience the brand offers, how it makes consumers feel, and to what extent it appeals to the sense organs have started to gain importance.

Product Marketing   Service Marketing   Experiential Marketing

Figure 2.7: The Evolution of Marketing

At this point, it is of pivotal importance to be the brand that was first associated with in the consumers' mind map when certain concepts come to their mind. For instance, the BMW brand comes to mind when the best engine to drive springs to mind, Volvo is the first brand that comes to mind when it comes to safety, or Mercedes represents prestige.

Brands attain a long-lasting place in the memory of the consumers as they enable consumers to go through experiences that convey their authentic promises in parallel with their positioning strategies. A good example of experiential marketing could be the "Roastery Experience" offered by the Starbucks brand in Seattle which is the city where the story of the brand was initiated. By the "Roastery Experience", the company offers its customers an experience supported by augmented reality (AR), thus, the customers can observe the adventures of the coffee from the very first stage till the moment it is brought to them.

Figure 2.8 Experiential Marketing: Starbucks Atmosphere

https://youtu.be/mq4GZBF1hOY

Experiential marketing is based on the idea that human beings have a heart along with their brain and they are beings that can feel. It is not possible for a brand to be humane or to have a character unless it addresses the human spirit. And, it is at this very point that Marketing 3.0 comes into play.

The concept of Marketing 3.0 is based on the thought that people are humans who have a mind, heart, and spirit, instead of treating them just as consumers. This concept explains that a brand should have values attached importance by its customers and those values are to be defended no matter what happens, in a way that forms an integrity in terms of the brand's mission, vision and operation steps.

In the face of information pollution and bombardment of messages from all brands, consumers opt for listening to the brands that have a different story regarding the basic problems of humanity, and that are environmentally-conscious with an aim to make this world more sustainable instead of solely focusing on making more profit at all costs. Other brands cannot even pass through the absolute perception threshold, that is, the perceptual filter, to be able to transmit the message...

The Evolution of Marketing

So, what kind of an evolutionary process has the marketing discipline undergone?

Over the past 60 years, marketing has evolved from being product-centered (Marketing 1.0) to being consumer-centered (Marketing 2.0). Today, marketing is now becoming completely human-centered (Marketing 3.0).

Marketing 1.0 refers to the product-centered age in which anything that was produced could easily be sold, which was a typical characteristic of the Industrial Revolution. At that stage, product management was at the heart... The marketing function was evaluated in a tactical fashion. As in the case of McCarthy's 4 Ps model, marketing was seen as a concept that consisted solely of product development, pricing, promotion, and distribution functions.[14]

Marketing 2.0 is characterized by the crisis environment in the 1970s and based on the fact that not everything that was produced could easily be sold, which shifted the focus over to the customers and their needs. At this stage, customer segmentation, targeting and positioning (STP) became the new processes in the marketing strategy.

Marketing 3.0 has emerged as a new trend against the endless economic turmoil on the global scale, fierce competition in the markets and the world becoming a more difficult place to live in. Consumers, who think that global brands which have a capitalist understanding to a large extent are the reason for the current situation the world has reached, have gradually lost their belief in the brands. The behaviors and values of companies attract the attention of consumers either in a positive or negative sense. In this regard, the question of whether brands have concerns about environmental issues and sustainability dimension is something that consumers carefully monitor.

What Does Marketing 3.0 Promise?

Today, people prefer brands that address their deepest needs concerning social, economic and environmental justice. Consumers do not only seek functional or emotional satisfaction in the products they choose, but they also ask for the satisfaction of the human spirit. Brands that successfully implement Marketing 3.0 have greater values to add to the world as they are willing to offer solutions concerning social problems. Marketing 3.0 brings the concept of marketing up to a level of human aspirations, values and spirit. Marketing 3.0 believes that people are holistic and that con-

---

[14] E. Jerome McCarthy, *Basic Marketing: A Managerial Approach,* McGraw-Hill/Irwin, 1978.

sumers' other needs and hopes should never be disregarded. Hence, Marketing 3.0 complements the notion of emotional marketing with human spirit marketing.

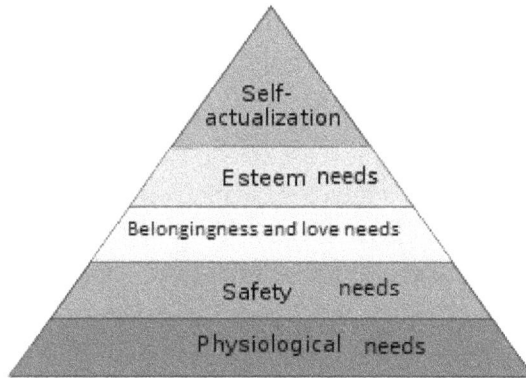

Figure 2.12: Maslow's Hierarchy of Needs

With the rise of the middle class and increase in welfare, today, beyond the functional and emotional satisfaction in Maslow's Hierarchy of Needs, the needs at the top of the pyramid, that is, the satisfaction of the human spirit, are sought. Accordingly, people would rather like to be a part of a cause and interact with brands that have been able to produce an intriguing story with a distinctive and authentic cause with the intent of making the world a better place.

In Marketing 3.0, where brand management is at the forefront, people prefer brands not because of their functional benefits, but because they express their worldview and the values they uphold. In other words, the brand becomes a means for self-expression. Within this framework, let us examine some of the successful examples of brands that have developed an authentic discourse for humanity.

You're more beautiful than you think.

Seeking an extraordinary campaign for personal care, the Dove brand has developed an extraordinary discourse for women, as they are its target audience, in accordance with the philosophy of Marketing 3.0. Through a number of research Dove conducted, the brand revealed that people did not find themselves beautiful at a striking ratio of 94%. Thus, the brand decided to tell women that they are more beautiful than they think in a striking way. With this in mind, the brand worked with an expert who had been responsible for drawing sketches of suspects based on witness statements in the FBI, the US Federal Bureau of Investigation. The expert asked the women who were behind a screen to describe their face, and then asked a different person who had seen that woman a few minutes ago to describe that woman. When the two drawings for the women were compared by bringing the drawings next to one another, the drawings made based on the description of other people always showed a more beautiful face whereas the drawings based on the description of the women themselves always portrayed a face that was sad and not so beautiful. Consumers showed a lot more attention to the message "You are more beautiful than you think", which is the essence of the brand's story, than what had been predicted. The video of the story soon went viral.

Figure 2.13: Marketing 3.0 and Dove - You are More Beautiful Than You Think

Figure 2.14: Marketing 3.0 and Dove - You are More Beautiful Than You Think

https://youtu.be/EDCGjFV2KCQ

Always like a Girl #AlwaysLikeAGirl

Always, a brand of feminine hygiene products, has found out that the expression 'like a girl' tends to have negative connotations in almost every part of the world and it implies despising. Deciding to develop a new discourse for humanity, the brand launched a new campaign with its #AlwaysLikeAGirl hashtag, in which its name was devised smartly as a Trojan horse. Accordingly, the brand invited everyone to challenge this perception, and argued that girls should come together to change this misconception. Having received much publicity, the campaign has caused a snowball effect, encouraging girls from all over the world to share the videos which display their best performances in all sorts of areas with the hashtag of the campaign on social media.

Figure 2.15: Marketing 3.0 and Always - Always Like a Girl

Figure 2.16: Marketing 3.0 and Always - Always Like a Girl

https://youtu.be/JM9XEus54bY

Marketing 3.0 and the Social Media Revolution

The main factors that make Marketing 3.0 possible are the technological platforms that have made production possible through a cooperative approach, devices such as computers and smartphones becoming more affordable worldwide with the penetration showing an upward trend and most importantly, the social media revolution.

Human beings, by nature, want to be connected with other people, not with companies. Consumers trust each other more than they trust companies. The rise of social media reflects that consumers' confidence has shifted from companies to other consumers exclusively. According to a study conducted by Nielsen Global, only a limited number of consumers tend to rely on the advertisements of companies. Approximately 92% of the respondents state that they trust the recommendations of their acquaintances; and 70% of consumers say that they believe in the consumer reviews posted on the Internet.[9]

In this case, it should be ensured that people can create communities within themselves communicating through word of mouth and that they can become a volunteer brand ambassador of certain brands, feeling that they are a part of a cause.

Marketing 3.0 refers to the age of horizontal communication in which vertical control does not work anymore. Here, only honesty, integrity, genuineness and authenticity will win.

Towards Illusional Marketing

The Profile of the Modern Customer: Extremely Busy and Disloyal
Loyalty is the willingness of a person –be it a client, an employee, or a friend - to make an investment and personal sacrifice to strengthen a relationship.[15] When we think of the customer, what it means is not leaving a brand that treats him / her well and gives him/her a good value in the long run, even if it does not offer the best price in a particular transaction. There have been two radical changes against the brand in this equation. First of all, the sacrifice expected from customers in the attention economy to take action, such as liking a brand on social media or participating in their campaigns, and so on, is not like it used to be in the old days. Under this information bombardment, it becomes increasingly harder for customers, whose time is more precious than their money, to bother to respond to your interaction request. Secondly, the rate of loyal customers is decreasing day by day. It is possible to explain this situation with both the

---

[15] Hong-bumm Kim, Woo Gon Kim, Jeong A. An, "The Effect of Consumer-Based Brand Equity on Firms' Financial Performance," *Journal of Consumer Marketing,* Vol. 20, 4/5 (2003), 335–351.
https://doi.org/10.1108/07363760310483694

increasing competition and the new generation consumers who are less loyal to brands

That being the case, brands are in need of new methods to convince their customers to interact in order to increase their loyalty. Illusional marketing, at this very point, leaves aside the conscious and questioning brain, which is already busy enough and needs a rest, and instead targets the *old brain, which works along with stimuli such as emotions, memories, stories, visuals and entertainment elements (games), and which is on autopilot, allowing us to act intuitively without having to think* and *which is the one that is, in effect, in charge of making the actual purchase decision.*

A customer whom you make feel good, or whom you reward with a badge, or in short, on whom you create a 'Wow' effect, may be someone who would not normally bat an eye, may actually become a volunteer ambassador of your brand even without being conscious about it. NikeFuel can be given as a successful example of this type of *'experience worth sharing'* design.

Designing Experiences Worth Sharing

NikeFuel is a good example of a brand transformation with the Nike brand growing into a brand that offers an entire experience expected from a sports equipment brand. This product is a digital wristband with a motion sensor that perceives all the activities of the user and monitors exactly how many calories the user burns. In addition to offering a smooth user experience, the activity area is not just a gym, but anywhere for users with this product that successfully applies the gamification mechanics. In this system, which invites you to compete with other users on how many calories are burned daily, monthly and yearly, in order to be the leader on a board or to achieve your daily goal, you can find yourself getting off the bus two stops earlier and running in the middle of the night. Even though the badge you have obtained for reaching the target is something virtual, this meaningful experience becomes one worth sharing on the way to a fit life; and what's more, the badge obtained on social media can be shared with everyone. In today's world in which brands cannot even make their loyal customers click the 'like' button on social media, the importance of making experiences worth sharing becomes more apparent.

Figure-2.17: Nike FuelBand

https://youtu.be/1r5YoWLexEc

We have pointed out that consumers are turning to those that make them feel good. Visualize a moment when you go to the cinema with your family. Productions in which the hero of the story shares the same values with you, or in which a core message is given at a time when you feel close to the hero, or which makes you say "Yes! That's it!" would make you feel good. Under such circumstances, you forget about the world outside and get immersed in the story, and if the production is really that good, then you will still be under its influence for a while even after leaving the cinema. Sometimes you would share the story and message of the film with your friends passionately. Many major brands in our age are trying to create this aura effect by using illusional techniques in marketing.

So, When Do Consumers Feel Good?

Consumers feel good when they become a part of a cause they attach importance to, when they deal with brands that value them as human beings rather than an entity to be exploited, and also when they go through unique experiences that are well-designed throughout, appealing to all senses as much as possible, that they cannot find elsewhere, and when they are immersed in the flow of things, losing track of time.

The New Weapons of Brands

We have mentioned earlier that digital is the new normal. The digital revolution causes an explosion in the amount of information produced. This leaves the brands with the attention economy, a kind of economy they have never encountered before. New tools have been added into the toolbox of the marketing professionals so that they can cope with this situation. These new tools which have all been developed by benefiting from the advantages of the digital world are of critical importance for differentiation and brand leadership in our era.

These weapons, each of which could be the subject matter of a separate book, are grouped into three main categories:

☐ The first and foremost strategy called *"Customer Development"* approach is for those who want to develop a product from scratch so that they can move away from 'average products' and develop the product that they consumers exactly want,

☐ The second one is *Growth Hacking*, with the new generation of analytical technologies in the search for optimum business model setup when the product does not change or could not be changed,

☐ Lastly, when it is not possible to make changes to the product and business model, brands opt for implementing the *Illusional Marketing* techniques.

This book focuses on illusional marketing techniques. Therefore, the other two approaches will be just briefly touched upon here. More information about these approaches can be found in the appendix of the book.

Table 2: The New Weapons of Brands in the Digital Age

Approach	Customer Development	Growth Hacking	Illusional Marketing
The Area of Application	Developing the product from scratch	It is not /may not be possible to change the product but innovation in the business model is possible	The product and business model is fixed
Problem	Inadequacy of the 'average' solutions as offered through 'Product Development'	Old approaches become ineffective in promoting the products	Difficulty in attracting the conscious attention of consumers
Aim	Giving customers what they exactly want	• Measuring every setup in the business model. • Developing self-selling products by setting up the optimum business model	Addressing the subconscious
Tool	Lean Start-up	New Generation of Analytical Technologies Sales Funnel Optimization	• Storytelling • User experience • Gamification

Method	Testing the basic assumptions about the business idea from the early stages as quickly and cheaply as possible	• Achieving maximum conversion rates by using a variety of innovative digital promotion strategies • Determining where the most profitable customers come from based on the "customer lifetime value" (CLV)	• The brand has a story that corresponds to customers, • Promising a smooth user experience, • A gamified product setup design that will be able to keep the motivation high
Focus	Value Engine Design	Growth Hacking, Lean Analytical Marketing Automation	Human-centric marketing and brand management
Related Concepts	Value proposition design Jobs-to-be-done Theory, Lean Start-up	Growth Hacking, Lean Analytical Marketing Automation	Behavioral Psychology, Marketing 3.0

References

9. Nielsen "Trust Barometer Report" http://www.nielsen.com/us/en/insights/reports-downloads/2012/global-trust-in-advertising-and-brand-messages.html Accessed Date: 23.09.2016.
10. Simon, Herbert A., "Designing Organizations for an Information-Rich World," in *Computers, Communications, and the Public Interest.* Baltimore: Johns Hopkins University Press, 1971.
11. Davenport, Thomas H., & Beck, John C. *The Attention Economy: Understanding the New Currency of Business.* Boston: Harvard Business School Press, 2001.
12. Schmitt, Bernd. "Experiential marketing," *Journal of Marketing Management, vol. 15, no. 1-3* (Apr. 1999), 53-67.
13. Toffler, Alvin. *Future Shock.* New York: Random House, 1970.
14. McCarthy, E. Jerome. *Basic Marketing: A Managerial Approach.* McGraw-Hill/Irwin, 1978.
15. Kim, Hongbumm, Kim, Woo Gon, & An, Jeong A. "The Effect of Consumer-Based Brand Equity on Firms' Financial Performance," *Journal of Consumer Marketing,* Vol: 20, 4/5 (2003), 335–351. https://doi.org/10.1108/07363760310483694

PART 3

ILLUSIONAL MARKETING

Thinking is hard and boring for many people. When it comes to making a decision, we tend to move in line with our intuitions rather than thinking in a rational way.

-- Dan Ariely, *Predictably Irrational*

Illusional marketing emerges from the fact that it is getting harder and harder to attract the consumers' conscious attention and is based on the idea of addressing the unconscious.

In this part of the book, we will analyze the concept of *illusion* before we move on to the concept of illusional marketing.

The Concept of Illusion

Illusion is known as the illusion regarding senses. People perceive the world through their five senses and illusion is a system that targets these sensory organs. Thus, illusion creates conditions in the person's mind that cannot be logically explained. Illusions can arise from visual techniques as well as cognitive or perceptual ones[16].

Illusional Marketing

Since the 1990s, particularly over the last two decades, psychologists have made significant discoveries on how the human brain works and the basic underlying mechanics of human behaviors. The critical importance of the unconscious, known as the right brain, has been proven through new evidence, for almost all the processes involved in, such as the moment a consumer comes across the brand for the first time, his / her interaction process, developing loyalty as well as all the other related processes.

The fact that Daniel Kahnemann, a scientist who had also studied psychology, won the 2002 Nobel Economy Prize with his mentioning of findings related to the unconscious in his book *Thinking, Fast and Slow* pinpointed the increasing importance of behavioral economics. The importance of this issue is verified in a similar fashion with the development that the 2017 Nobel Prize was also won by a behavioral economics professor, Thaler, who based his book entitled *Nudge* (2016) on the idea that consumers are not rational beings. The trend that started with psychology and went along with economics has continued to be influential in the marketing discipline as well over the recent years. Neuromarketing attempts to explain this phenomenon by examining the signals in the brain. Yet, such approaches remain to be on tactical dimension so it becomes necessary to examine the impact of behavioral psychology and unconscious on marketing at a strategic dimension which is beyond the tactical dimension that such approaches mostly rest upon. This book provides a proposal of a model through conceptualization under the name of illusional marketing by examining storytelling, gamification and user experience design techniques from different disciplines that have been resorted to frequently over the recent years and are all directed towards the unconscious, specifically towards the primitive brain.

In a world where the products and services have become similar to each other, the new competitive environment has emerged, based on the

---

[16] Patricia Pisters, *The Neuro-Image: A Deleuzian Film-Philosophy of Digital Screen Culture*. Stanford University Press, 2012.

principle of making consumers have smooth experiences. Today, the ultimate level marketing has reached is one at which consumers wish to act without putting any mental effort, If possible act without thinking at all, throughout almost all the stages of marketing, beginning with the first moment they meet the brand, continuing with forming interaction and developing loyalty for repeated purchases. Illusional marketing has lent a hand to marketers in today's world that is characterized by the attention economy through which it is a lot more difficult than in the past to attract the active attention of consumers.

Illusional Marketing goes beyond experiential marketing, presenting the consumers, who demand more and more from the brands, a world of illusion which makes them feel good while entertaining them and does not require consumers to spend mental effort. In short, such a state is called a flow state.

Illusional marketing, just like experiential marketing, targets the senses in compliance with the marketing aims. Similar to neuromarketing, illusional marketing aims at engaging the consumer in an interaction with the brand as a result of the stimulation of the old brain, which is to do with senses and regarded as the unconscious brain, through a particular systematic so that the consumer will act in the desired manner and direction. By gamifying real life plot which is not a game or in other words by imitating a game, it enables consumers to be more motivated while using the product, taking the desired actions and making repeated purchases. This evokes completely different feelings in the consumers while connecting the brand with a story that directly relates to the values in the consumers' imagination. Thus, it makes the consumers enter a kind of an imaginary world by designing the user experience in a way that does not make them think, but that allows them to have fun, while they forget about themselves, and as a consequence, feel in the flow. With the development of the AR and VR technologies, these weapons which are available for the brands have become much more powerful in the name of user experience.

Resting upon the fact that it is getting harder and harder to attract the conscious attention of consumers, illusional marketing is based on the thought of addressing the unconscious.

> *Humans prefer to do their daily errands without coming to a decision.*
> *-- B. J. Fog, Habit Designer, Stanford*

From Experiential Marketing to Illusional Marketing

Figure 3.11 summarizes the difference in approach with regard to some basic dimensions among traditional marketing, experiential marketing and illusional marketing. In this context, the information conveyed for the experiential marketing and illusional marketing in the end expressed an extended version of the relevant concept and carried it to a much different dimension rather than replacing the approach in traditional marketing.

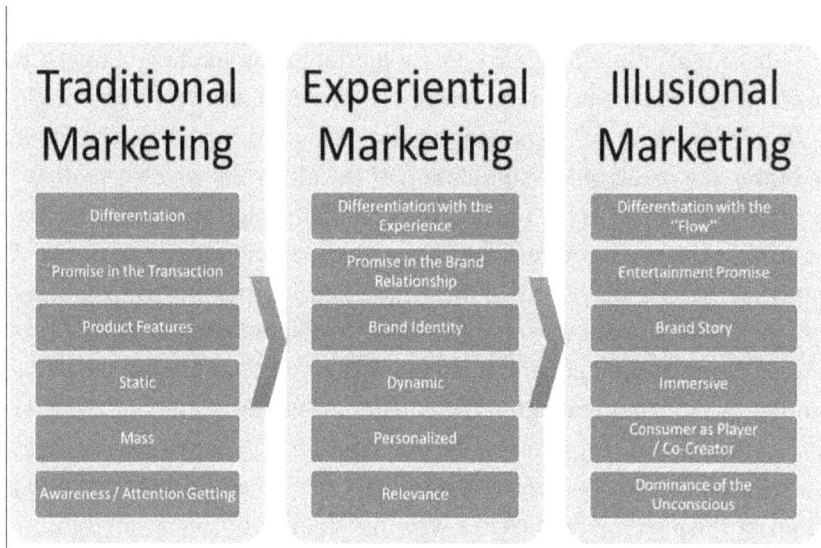

Traditional Marketing	Experiential Marketing	Illusional Marketing
Differentiation	Differentiation with the Experience	Differentiation with the "Flow"
Promise in the Transaction	Promise in the Brand Relationship	Entertainment Promise
Product Features	Brand Identity	Brand Story
Static	Dynamic	Immersive
Mass	Personalized	Consumer as Player / Co-Creator
Awareness / Attention Getting	Relevance	Dominance of the Unconscious

Figure 3.1 Marketing Approaches from Traditional to Illusional
Source: adapted from Khan's [17] model.

Differentiation → Differentiation with Experience → Differentiation with the "Flow"

---

[17] Barbara E. Kahn, *Global Brand Power: Leveraging Branding for Long-Term Growth*. Wharton Digital Press, 2013.

The most important principle of traditional marketing is differentiation in competition. In experiential marketing, this concept is extended targeting differentiation along with all the dimensions of the presented experience. The presented experience should appeal not only to the mind, but also to the senses and heart too. The ideal one would be appealing to all of our five senses while addressing the senses. In brief, if the brand has a particular smell, taste, color, visual and voice, it will be more possible for the brand to have a more long-lasting and impressive significance in the mind and heart of the consumers. For example, the fragrance produced by Singapore Airlines[18] produced specifically for the brand is not only used on the planes, this fragrance is also used in all the agencies of the airline company across the globe. The airline provides a unique experience to its customers, and the moment these loyal customers of the airline take a step in the agency, they start to go through the experience of the airline and being on board owing to this fragrance. Equally, a lot of textile brands have started to make use of fragrances peculiar to their brand in their retail stores, which shows that this action is a product of a similar strategy.

In illusional marketing, differentiation is aimed by carrying the experience one step further and immersing the consumers into a flow state. As has been explained in Csikszentmihalyi's[19] "flow theory", if someone does something she enjoys doing, based on her intuitions and habits that have turned out to be an automatic behavioral pattern without being required to think about it, then she will be taken with a flow state, thus, she will not realize how time flies. This extreme point which is also desired in games, stories as well as in experience design is the flow state itself.

Commitment in Shopping → Commitment in Brand Relationship → Commitment to Entertain

---

[18] Susan Carey, "Airlines Try Signature Fragrances, but Not Everyone Is on Board," *Wall Street Journal,* 1 Feb. 2015. https://www.wsj.com/articles/airlines-try-signature-fragrances-but-not-everyone-is-on-board-1422832562 accessed 12 May 2018.

[19] Mihaly Csikszentmihalyi & Isabella S. Csikszentmihalyi (eds.), *Optimal Experience: Psychological Studies of Flow in Consciousness,* Cambridge University Press, 1992.

In traditional marketing, the focal point used to be the single operation / transaction marketing promise where value shopping between the buyer and the seller was realized. However, as time went by, the significance of relationship marketing that is oriented towards the development of long-term relations with the customers started to be grasped. Consequently, this approach, which lies at the heart of the customer relations management, has been adopted in many of the marketing operations. Experiential marketing emphasizes the importance of commitment in this relationship. As for illusional marketing, consumers make their preferences based on the extent that the brand they are evaluating makes them feel good or whether those brands offer them entertainment or not. Deriving from this, the elimination of boring or mentally exhausting steps is a part of the commitment to entertain. To illustrate, Apple brand pledges an experience that literally makes the users feel good and entertains them with respect to the external design of its products and use of operating systems. According to many Apple users, the experience that Apple allows them to go through becomes a reason for preference since Apple products are less mentally exhausting and spare the user from unnecessary details when they are compared with Android products.

Product Features → Brand Personality → Brand Story

In the past, it sufficed for brands just to bring to the fore their product features in order to sell a product that had been developed. Yet, it also became a requirement for the brand to have a personality in experiential marketing. Moving from the fact that brand personality is not sufficient per se in illusional marketing, brands make a story of the competitive environment they are in and render the values they fight for, their targets and the enemy figure into a story format. Eventually, it is through this way that they can ensure communication with all the stakeholders, which are appreciated much more by the consumers. In the example of Apple, brand customers have an outlook for life, an enemy figure that adopts a formal lifestyle, resistant to change, maintaining the status quo. That is to say, there is also the story. Since this story has reached people and found its correspondence through this story, many fanatics of the brand got utterly shocked when Steve Jobs, namely the real hero of the brand died. As a result, Apple stores became common places for many people who left flowers in memory of Steve Jobs whose death had a shocking impact on the Apple fanatics.

Static Experience → Dynamic Experience → Immersive Experience

Contrary to traditional marketing, experiential marketing engages consumers in an interactive manner. For example, a female customer who enters one of the Channel stores finds the opportunity to have the experience of applying the products on her face and body rather than coming across a static presentation of the sales representative. In illusional marketing concept, the idea is to make the user feel good by enabling her to be entertained with the help of technologies such as augmented-reality (AR) and virtual reality (VR). As such consumers feel in the flow, get away from real life for a while and are literally immersed into the experience that is promised. The plot and characters of the story, the consumers within the framework of the rules of the game assume a different kind of personality. An e-sports company, Zwift is a good example of this phenomenon. As an alternative to traditional fitness equipment, Zwift cycling platform gives the cyclists the opportunity to compete with other real people in virtual reality (VR) platform from their home. The gamified platform also simulates a real outdoor training environment.

Zwift VR Based Cycling Platform
Video: https://youtu.be/cP_CcX_uOdo

Mass Marketing → Individualized Marketing → Co-Creator / Player

Mass production and mass marketing approaches used to be predominant in traditional marketing. However, in experiential marketing, it is essential to focus on experience on an individual basis, and on customized presentation as much as possible. In the view of illusional marketing, co-creation and prosumer (producing consumer) understanding is relevant, which goes beyond doing presentation to the consumers at an individual level. To that end, it is possible to make consumers be disguised in the role of the producer and contributor in line with what the brand desires through the realization of the gamified mechanism design.

Threadless.com is a good example of consumers' playing co-creator role. The website sells T-shirts, accessories etc. with authentic visuals. The platform challenges everyone with authentic design ideas to submit their designs to their platform and let others rate and vote those ideas. Having received constructive feedback from others, the designers submit their final visuals to the system for final election. Crowds vote and select the winning ideas. The website adds the winning designs to their portfolio. The designer of the visual gets a commission for every item sold with her visuals on it. This gamified co-creation process is very beneficial to the brand. Because, the crowds who select the winning ideas are also those who buy the actual products.

Awareness → Relevance → Dominance of the Unconscious

In traditional marketing, it would suffice for the initiation of the communication process if the brand raised awareness. However, in experiential marketing it became critical that the consumers related the brand discourse to their own values and matched up the discourse with their values. At the last stage marketing has reached, techniques that address the unconscious are used and approaches that involve the consumers in the process automatically and as a matter of course are applied, which do not necessitate any awareness at all. Given the fact that consumers' attention and time are more scarce than ever in the attention economy, this approach has a very powerful and disruptive impact. Brands can kill two birds with one stone with this strategy. On the one hand, it becomes possible to bypass the consumers' critical and questioning left brain. On the other hand, consumers prefer this kind of interaction more than the alternatives because this enables them to save their valuable attention and time. In brief, habits have an extraordinary effect in our lives. This is because the human brain is inclined to transfer anything it can to the autopilot mode, and by doing so, it gets rid of load and burden. For example, navigation applications such as Yandex Navi have become such an inseparable part of our daily lives that some people have started to use this application even when they are heading for home. This technology which does not necessitate any thinking or reasoning on behalf of the user regarding the directions enables us to act in autopilot mode. Yet, it inevitably makes us totally shocked if our phone battery is dead. It is possible to observe that these techniques have gradually entered into all areas of our lives in the long-run. Here, the critical point is that there are instances in which conscious awareness is also significant, and it is required that illusional marketing techniques be analyzed considering all of its dimensions along with some of its negative side effects and downsides including their ethical dimension as well.

Why Illusion?

There are a few reasons why this concept is named particularly illusional marketing.

1) Illusional Marketing is a Typical Example of Cognitive Illusion.

When explaining the function of the unconscious Kahneman states that the concept of illusion that conveys the meaning of deception is not only at a visual dimension but it also includes the "cognitive illusion dimension". While explaining this concept, he makes an allusion to a story a Professor in a Faculty of Medicine tells his students while lecturing... According to the story, an old lady coming to the clinic for her examination starts talking immediately right after she sits down and says "I have been to three doctors before coming here and no one has understood me. Whatever I told them, however I told them, they did not seem to understand me, but you look different. You seem to be listening to me..." The Professor advises his students to tell the patient to get out of the room immediately in such a situation because the patient has put forth a story and placed you in the middle of the story, making you the protagonist or the hero. It is so difficult for you to get rid of this situation... It is impossible to deny this kind of

69

power stories have. In similar fashion, imagine that you are the chairman of a conglomerate. That day you are going to listen to two different project proposals from two different people on a significant issue and approve one of the proposals. Your nephew is one of those who will present one of the proposals, and the other presenter is one of your professional employees... Even if you try to be impartial, you cannot avoid a cognitive illusion in such a case...We, humans, inevitably experience the cognitive illusion in stories where there is a protagonist and those we identify ourselves with as well as in games we are wholly absorbed in and drifted by...

2) Illusional Marketing is the Last Stage which the Never-ending Desires of Consumers have Reached

Consumers now ask the brands to meet many tasks in their name, and while doing that, they want everything to be realized automatically and intuitively, without thinking or getting tired, without having to exert any effort, as if the automatic pilot mode is on. Kahneman's evaluation about marketing and consumer habits summarizes the whole thing: ***the more we humans produce, the more we consume and the more we ask for...The faster we get a service, we expect to get even a faster one... The easier the experience we undergo gets, the more we notice how easy it can get further...The more our extraordinary expectations are met, the more extraordinary expectations we begin to have...***

3) The Negative Connotation with respect to Illusion Holds True for the Ethical Dimension of Illusional Marketing

At the last stage that has been attained in the 21st century's post-modern marketing world, these new weapons available for the brands which guide consumers to consume more even if they do not need are in fact very effective in channelizing the consumers to behave in compliance with what the brands desire. What's more, consumers act without being aware of their behaviors through such weapons. This necessitates a thorough analysis of the issue in terms of "illusion" world marketing ethics. For example, Foursquare, in its early years, immediately became a product everyone was "playing" with the help of the competition created among "players", dashboards, distribution of badges such as the ones like the "mayor" of the location. After a while, people started to ask themselves

"What am I doing?, "How come have I run idly after such a futile thing? " In addition, many articles and reviews were published that revealed the particular situation. Right at this time, Foursquare company started to falter severely. After a long and turbulent period when the company was on the verge of dissolution, Foursquare decided to split the product into two different apps with the names Swarm and Foursquare. They decided to continue their path in that way. In short, gamification always works. However, if gamification merely aims at increasing the company's profit without intending to provide a long-term added value to the consumers, then the adopted strategy is doomed to boomerang or backfire after a while.

It frequently comes on the agenda that this is a natural result of a process designed meticulously down to the last detail by platform producers for the sake of making more money in a world where technology addiction is not coincidental and where the attention economy is felt profoundly. [20]

The Autopilot Strategy Model

The autopilot strategy model explains the theoretical infrastructure of illusional marketing. Many studies conducted in recent years have revealed the critical importance of behavior patterns in the purchase behavior.[21,22]

---

[20] Adnan V. Ertemel, "Implications of Blockchain Technology on Marketing," *Journal of International Trade, Logistics and Law, 4*:2 (2018), pp. 35-44.
[21] Charles Duhigg, *The Power of Habit: Why We Do What We Do in Life and Business,* Random House, 2012.
[22] Elizabeth A. Phelps, "Emotion and cognition: Insights from studies of the human amygdala," *Annu. Rev. Psychol. 57* (Jan 2006), pp. 27-53.

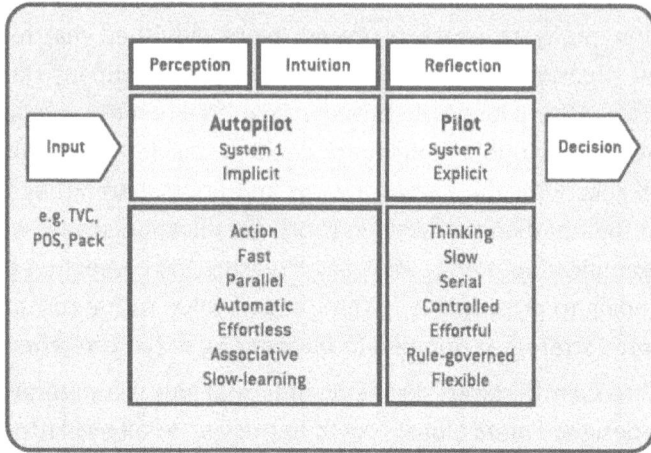

Figure 3.2: Kahneman's System 1 and System 2 Models.
Source: Kahneman(2000)

In System 1 and System 2 approach Kahneman developed about the way the human brain works, it was portrayed that the behaviors in the autopilot mode make up the overwhelming majority of the daily routine behaviors. The autopilot behavior, called System-1 defines the behaviors performed unconsciously and as a reflex, which do not require attention. For cases which System-1 cannot cope with, System-2, that is to say the active and conscious brain, intervenes. Being inclined to get rid of workload, our brain tries to sort out as many tasks as possible under the control of System-1 without getting exhausted.

As the businesses had more difficulty in their marketing activities to persuade consumers to interact, an alternative perspective in this regard was developed by Martin and Morich. They designed a new consumer behavior model along the path Kahneman had paved, claiming that consumer behavior is realized under the hegemony of the unconscious rather than being the outcome of a rationally thinking brain, which used to be the case acknowledged in the past.[23]

---

[23] Neale Martin & Kyle Morich, "Unconscious mental processes in consumer choice: Toward a new model of consumer behavior," *Journal of Brand Management* 18:7 (2011), pp. 483-505.

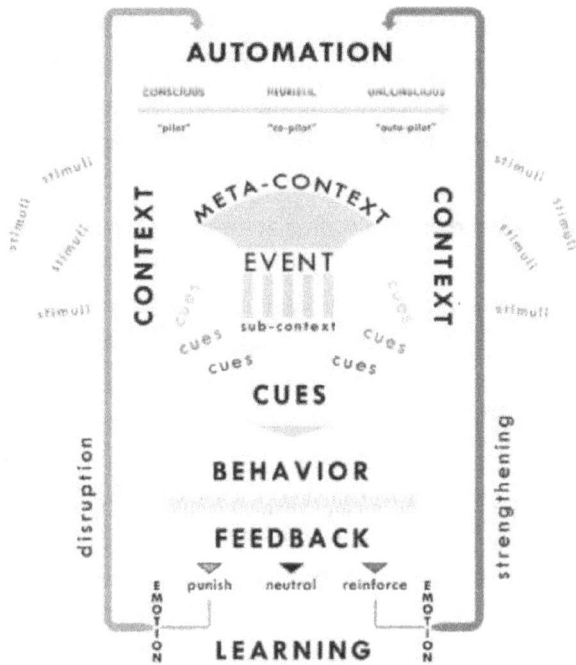

Figure 3.3: Martin-Morich model of consumer behavior.
Source: Martin and Morich(2011)

The autopilot strategy model that was developed on the basis of the two models in question explains the situation where the purchase behavior occurs under the control of System-1 Model through the techniques of gamification, storytelling and experience design with the complete use of the primitive brain's language. The process that starts off with the stimulus assumes the function of trigger and leads to the entry of a habit cycle, thus enables the realization of the autopilot behavior in an unconscious way. The consumer behavior at the end of this process may be a purchase decision or it may also appear as interaction and loyalty.

The behavioral patterns in the autopilot enable the brain to be relieved from mental intensity and help it get rid of the load. Thus, our brain can perform many activities simultaneously in a parallel fashion without requiring active attention. An example of an autopilot behavior would be an experienced driver, who has been driving for many years, speaking with others present in the car while driving through his / her automatic reflexes.

Thinking, making a decision and spending money... These phenomena basically cause pain to the human brain... Through techniques such as storytelling, user experience and gamification, brands manage to get consumers to engage in interaction without consumers being aware of the process.

User experience basically aims at enabling the consumer experience to be realized in a smooth way and based on intuitions, without causing the brain to become exhausted. While getting some money out of our pockets and spending it may give us pain, using a credit card alleviates this pain for a certain amount of time. Contactless payment makes this process even smoother. While brands were reflecting upon how they could enhance the consumers' payment processes, Uber company asked the question "what if we removed the payment step entirely", and they removed the payment entirely from the visible aspect of the process. As a result of this action, Uber has started to offer a more pleasant experience for its customers.

Gamification refers to the capability of motivating consumers toward interaction and using the products and services in a repeated manner, which is the biggest real life problem of our day.

It can be stated that almost everyone aged around 21 is an expert in playing games, considering the fact that we have grown up with games since babyhood, and based on Malcolm Gladwell's[24] principle that explains the requirement of doing practice of at least 10,000 hours to be able to master a certain skill and become the expert of that. Moving on from this fact, brands are capable of motivating the consumers automatically by gamifying their processes without the need of further explanation and discarding the unnecessary applications like a user's guide. It should be noted that gamification is to be implemented at the last stage, following the steps of storytelling and user experience design, and if the need arises. These strategies and their respective order can be explained with the metaphor of a car driving on the highway. While the destination of the journey refers to the story dimension, issues such as how safe the highway is, and whether it was designed in a way convenient for speeding or not refers to the user experience dimension. If the car does not speed up even if these

[24] Malcolm Gladwell, *Outliers: The Story of Success,* Little, Brown, 2008.

stages have been worked on, a motivating design or gamification intervenes so as to step hard on the acceleration ... Even though gamification always works in the short term, for it to work in the long term, the fact if it adds value to the consumers in real sense rather than adding value to the brand should be inquired and taken into account. Applications such as pedometers can be given as examples of meaningful gamification that can really offer added value and are sustainable too.

Contrary to the left hemisphere of the human brain which represents the critical and conscious part, establishing communication by using alternative techniques addressing the unconscious and exceeding the wall of logic is an approach that has been used recently. Likewise, neuro-marketing is concerned with which situations the human brain reacts in an irrational manner. However, it is necessary to analyze the concepts of storytelling, gamification and user experience, all of which concern the right hemisphere of the brain and whose efficiency have been approved, holistically in terms of marketing and brand strategy.

Today, the brands that have a story which is well-aligned with and nurtures the consumers' value system can differentiate themselves in the competition meaning regarding humanity. Storytelling is related to the formation of the brand identity at the strategic dimension and brand positioning. Following storytelling and user experience design, gamification design can be implemented for the motivation concerning the realization of the targeted behavior change if needed.

Pattern Recognition Capability in Autopilot

In all the aforementioned techniques, pattern perception capability and habit loop on the autopilot are at stake as one of the most basic dynamics of the subconscious. In this cycle, the brain is initially triggered by a cue and a certain routine is realized. If the routine has ended up with a reward, the behavior begins to turn out to be an increasingly indispensable one. The loop that is constantly encountered in storytelling is the never-ending journey of the protagonist.[25] In user experience, if the autopilot behavior has enabled the "job to be done"[26] to be performed easily without exerting effort, then saving effort and time is a reward for the brain, and it reinforces the behavior on the autopilot. The reward (like badge, score, etc.) given in gamification in exchange for behavior change and engaging in interaction by reinforcing the behavior in question becomes a habit that is not to be given up. To illustrate, a consumer entering a restaurant or a similar place firstly checks-in on Foursquare application because of being accustomed to the behavior by means of gamification .

The common denominators of the aforementioned techniques are that in all of them, the brain realizes a habit loop with which it is familiar and the sense of time is eliminated within the process.

Predictable, Routine Habit Loop

At the **dimension of loop**, in every story, as Campbell has put it, the cycle of the never-ending journey of the protagonist is experienced. The principal aim in gamification is the reinforcement of the desired behavior with a reward and transformation of the routine into a habit. On the other hand, what is targeted in user experience is the brain's getting rid of the burden as a result of doing the job to be done in an intuitive way and changing the very same job into a behavior on autopilot with this reward for the next time.

Elimination of the Sense of Time: *The Flow State*

Being unaware of how time has passed, in other words, losing sense of time, confirms the existence of a successful plot both in stories and gamification. Good stories activate the mirror neurons and by doing so, such stories teleport the audience to a completely different place and time. Games enable the consumers to have a different identity by leading them to assume a different role and responsibility. In the case of user experience, the ultimate target is the flow state, as Csikszentmihaly puts it: a state where one is not aware of how time has passed.

---

[25] Joseph Campbell, *The Hero with a Thousand Faces,* Pantheon, 1949.
[26] Clayton M. Christensen & Michael E. Raynor, *The Innovator's Solution: Creating and Sustaining Successful Growth,* Harvard Business School Press, 2003.

Illusional Marketing Acid Test

An acid Test can be defined as testing a formula or concept that has been put forward on an extreme example to see whether it works even under that particular extreme circumstance or not. The best way to understand whether you have come up with a good plot or not is to try your product on a small child.

Meet Your New Test Team!

Your product should do the following to the extent that even a child can understand:

İllusional Marketing Acid Test

Meet Your New Test Team!

Should tell a story which is imprinted in the minds (Storytelling)

Could be used without requiring active thought (User Experience)

Should motivate to engage in interaction (Gamification)

Figure 3.4 Illusional Marketing Acid Test: Children

Children listen to stories with undivided attention and they are impressed by stories they can relate to themselves. What's more, they never forget such stories either. Perhaps the only way to convey a message to a child effectively is to tell a story. Nothing is more powerful for a brand than a story which can also correspond to children, is authentic and intriguing while relating to humanity.

> *Approaches such as neuro-marketing are gaining more and more significance, and it has been acknowledged that the subconscious play a primary role in the consumers' purchase decisions.*

As the second dimension of illusional marketing, user experience refers to the capability of a child to use a product even for the first time in an intuitive way, without having the need to think about it.

It is possible to see a good example of this in today's world with the features called Apps that can be installed on smartphones. For instance, it used to be inevitable even for a knowledgeable adult accountant to resort to the help menu instantly once a typical accounting application was installed on the desktop computers which were equipped with Windows. The fact that even kids can easily use the applications on smartphones in an intuitive manner, sensing what everything is and how it works proves that these applications have a good user experience design. User experience, the ultimate objective of which can be summarized as "design that does not make you think" appears as a relatively new and multidisciplinary movement that is becoming increasingly more significant.

Finally, we may say that almost all kids get excited when they hear the suggestion "Let's play a game" and they automatically get motivated to display the desired behavior no matter what that behavior is. Children will also inevitably and naturally be motivated when they experience a gamified mechanism design that will encourage your customers to manifest the desirable behavior you want them to display as the brand.

> *"The more we produce, the more we consume and the more we ask for*
>
> *The faster we receive something, we expect to receive an even faster one.*
>
> *The easier it gets, the more we notice how easier it can get..*
>
> *The more our extraordinary expectations are met, the more extraordinary requests we begin to make.."*
>
> **- Daniel Kahneman**

Let us now analyze some successful applications that enable intuitive use without the need for thinking even for a kid who does not know how to read and has not even learned how to speak yet.

iPhone–Compass Application

Even a brand like Apple who places enhancing the user experience in the center of its story, was far from being good in terms of user experience at the beginning. The standard compass application on the iPhone products used to give directions to its users with a written notification stating that users had to draw the ∞ sign by their hands so that the compass could be activated. However, with the user interface developed later, it gamified this process asking the users to turn a ball around the circle and encouraging them to increase the lines around the ball. In the end, the behavior that had been expected to be performed by the users through a directive in the previous bad experience design was altered so that the same behavior would be performed by the user both through gamification and an experience design that does not make you think.

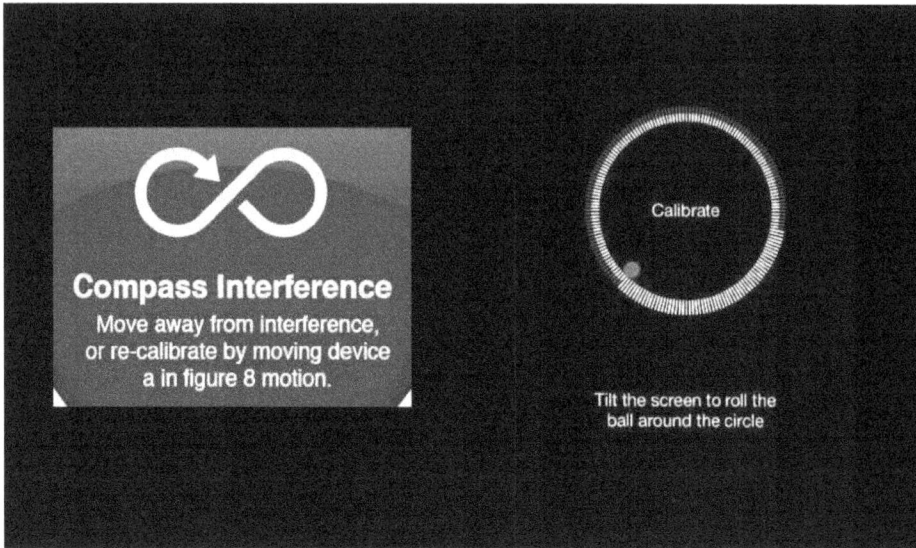

Figure 3.5: The Old vs. New Version of the Compass Interface on iPhone that has been Gamified Offering an Experience that does not Make You Think

Augmented Reality (AR) Application that Teaches Coding with a Magic Wand

Harry Potter Kano Coding Kit, which entails the elements of a game and entertainment, enables children and youngsters to learn to code using a magic wand, by drawing them in a Harry Potter story all at once. The application that enables a rod similar to a wand to interact with tablet applications and draws the user in a virtual world with the augmented reality technology encompasses all the elements of illusional marketing.

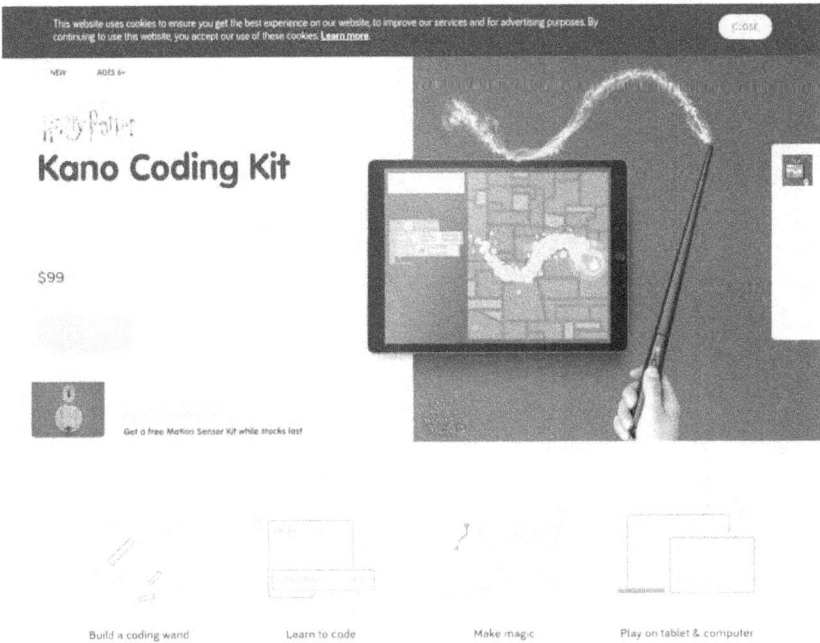

Figure 3.6: Harry Potter Kano Coding Kit

https://youtu.be/Jq6ltwjPMdl

You can use the QR code to watch the Harry Potter Kano Coding experience.

The Smart Insole

Another example is a Bluetooth enabled smart insole product designed in a way that even a child who has not yet learned how to read and write can use. The Lechal brand insole can be thought of as a different type of navigation device for pedestrians. It works in an integrative manner with the application on the phone and the user gets the directions through the vibration of the insole. When it is required to turn right , the insole on the right vibrates, if the user has to take a turn to the left, then the one on the left will vibrate. If both insoles vibrate, it means you have reached your destination.

Bluetooth enabled Insoles

NAVIGATE · INTERACT · STAY FIT

Figure 3.7: A Successful User Experience Example - Lechal Vibrating Insole

Another example we may provide on this matter is a smartphone application called AccuWeather application which is concerned with weather forecasts. When you open the application, the weather condition in your location appears on the screen along with visuals only, almost without any captions at all, and which does not require additional explanation either. The user experience particularly on the mobile platforms is currently heading towards this very direction. A user experience design in which universal visuals and signifiers are easily comprehended by almost all countries' citizens rather than the written explanations comes to the fore.

Figure 3.8 The Universal Language of the Visuals in
Mobile User Experience – AccuWeather

An Acid Test of Instagram's User Experience on an Animal

The video below demonstrates Instagram exemplary user experience. The user experience of the app is so intuitive that even a Chimpanzee can use it without any fuss or bother. Note that the right brains of human beings are very similar to those of animals. Therefore, animals can also be used as acid test for such techniques.

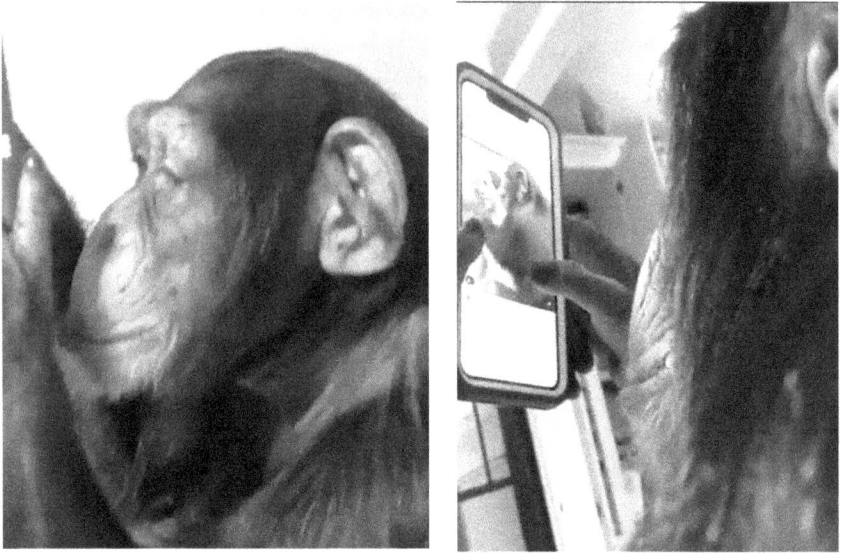

Figure 3.9 A Chimpanzee as an acid test for Instagram user experience
https://youtu.be/CyNnR4Nxddc

Blockchain and Crypto Projects as an Illusion

In this section, we will analyze the position and significance of the illusional techniques, storytelling, gamification and user experience in the Blockchain based world of the future. This analysis will be based on relevant examples.

The Blockchain revolution expresses a revolution that is as foundational as the Internet revolution. The reason we call it a foundational revolution, instead of using the adjective 'disruptive' is that most of the disruptive revolutions to be built on the Blockchain technology have not even been imagined yet, in Vitalik Buterin's terms, the founder of Ethereum... The Blockchain technology in essence completes the most important link missing on the Internet, and that missing link is the trust link. This technology enables the exchange of money and value on the Internet by solving the issue of trust at the protocol level.

Firstly, let us examine the token concept on which crypto projects are built.

The Concept of Token

Token can be named as a digital entity or money. Token, including loyalty score and all the other related concepts represents an entity that gives the entitlement of being involved in a network. Besides that, this entity is one that cannot be copied or is not lost. Bitcoin miners are rewarded with a certain number of bitcoins in return for the effort they have made and the energy they have worked off. In token economy, the rewarding mechanism which encourages different stakeholders, like the producers or users as a part of a society, to perform the desired behavior has become such a one that has been embedded into the system.

Storytelling and Gamification in Crypto Projects

Having come to life through thousands of crypto projects, the token economy can be deemed as one of the world's biggest socio-economic experiments today. The interesting point regarding this matter is that it has caught on, and tens of billions of dollars today that flow from individuals of all parts of the world are invested in such projects most of which are merely nothing but a dream. As a matter of fact, the overwhelming majority of the crypto projects only sells a dream as of 2018. In addition, it is projected that most of these projects will have become part of our daily lives by the mid-2020s. However, among a myriad of projects that aim at doing the same task, there are still people who believe in the *story* of a certain project and the future of it. These individuals are hell-bent and by purchasing the project token at a very low price, either at the initial stage of the project or sometimes at only ICO (Initial Coin Offering Level which refers to the first stage at which the crypto project gets funded) or at some times at a subsequent stage, they believe they have made a profitable attempt since they think that they have gained a price benefit, a price which is much more than the one they think the project will reach and be awarded with in the future. By doing so, they aim at being a part of the promised vision. Subsequently, owing to the fact that they believe in it and have the motivation of gaining financial return, they try to persuade everyone in their circle that the project is promising and has a bright future. In the end, when the number of people who believe in the project and those actually purchasing it increases along with the stock market value of the project going up, the financial returns of those who become the partners of the project at the initial stage also increase. And this new concept is called "network ownership effect" [27].

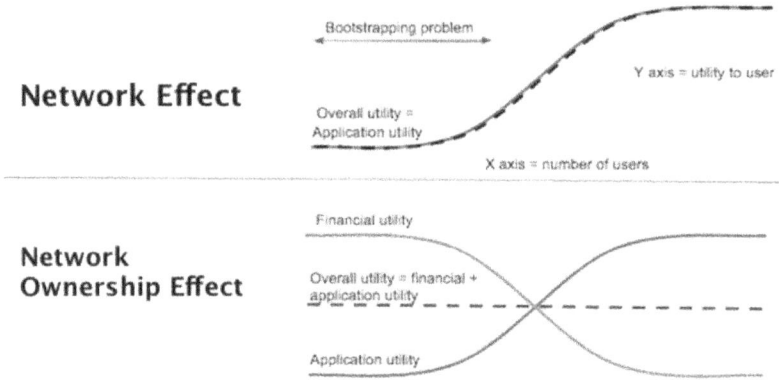

Network Effect

Bootstrapping problem

Y axis = utility to user

Overall utility = Application utility

X axis = number of users

Network Ownership Effect

Financial utility

Overall utility = financial + application utility

Application utility

Figure 3.10: The Network Ownership Effect in Crypto Projects

In a normal network effect, the higher the number of network members is, the higher the value of the network will be. Ownership of an email address, WhatsApp, or platforms such as sahibinden.com and eBay with their two-sided market position constantly make use of the network effect. In order for the network effect to be effective, it is required that the number of members exceeds a certain threshold value. Otherwise, the network will not be appealing at all. As for the network ownership, the mechanism works slightly differently. At the initial stage of the project, the stakeholders buy the *story* even when there are only a few members. These stakeholders gain token with the drive of ensuring financial return due to the fact that the token unit price is low, and hence, they act as the disciples of the project in this way. As the stock market value of the token increases in time, the amount of the financial return goes down. Yet, the network effect is realized owing to the effect of the increasing number of members. This new equation enables the funding of hundreds of crypto-projects that were only dreams at ICO level and the following stages by masses and the collecting of funds that are a great deal above what is in

---

[27] Chris Dixon, "Crypto Tokens: A Breakthrough in Open Network Design," *Medium*, 1 Jun 2017. https://medium.com/@cdixon/cryptotokens-a-breakthrough-in-open-network-design-e600975be2ef

fact needed. To illustrate the network ownership, La'Zooz Project, a competitor of Uber which is a centralized entity, may be explained. In this project, in which a totally decentralized structure is at stake, drivers gain tokens named Zooz instead of cash in return of the services they offer. The drivers who did not make any distinction between cash money and token at first, later tried to make the drivers and customers around them believe in the project spreading it with word-of-mouth communication naturally to maximize the financial return as their token accumulated. As a result, the increase in the token price has enabled all the stakeholders to gain a financial profit. Projects like Storj, Steemit and Kik come to the fore as crypto projects in which mechanism design and *gamification* are smartly developed and constructed. In these projects, ecosystem stakeholders offer services, produce content and cause a viral effect, and they are encouraged and rewarded with the tokens.

Building Strong Communities Through Collaborative Tokenized Ecosystems

Bitcoin itself is also a product of such a kind of mechanism design. In the notable article written by Satoshi Nakamoto, it is stated that what is different and original was not the cryptography or peer2peer logic that had already existed for decades. The principal original hypothesis of Satoshi Nakamoto is that if plenty of people believe in this, it will be impossible to break the system and its value will also exponentially increase with the number of members increasing. The underlying rationale behind bitcoin mining is that in exchange for doing the job the system requires, the reward is the bitcoin.

In brief, the new generation consumers want to work for projects in which they will not only be on the consumer side, but ones which will allow them to be on the producing and winning side. These projects are the ones whose story and meaning it entails they believe in, consequently, they want to be a part of such projects. These consumers find it boring to work for an institution on a full-time basis, which is a conventional way of earning money. Therefore, they would rather work for such projects and earn just enough money to be able to make a living. Shared office spaces are the ideal location for new generation producing consumers. Crypto-projects are also a perfect fit for the expectations of those prosumers.

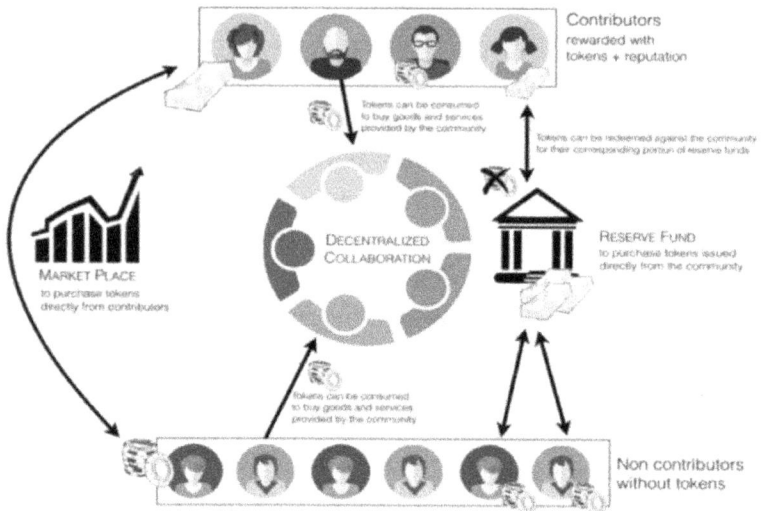

Figure 3.11: Decentralized Collaboration Model Ertemel(2018)28

The Importance of User Experience in Cryptoprojects

In the Blockchain vision, it is expected that various sectors like banking, communication, marketing and retailing will undergo changes in a disruptive way, and crypto-projects, like the pieces of Legos complementing one another, will dominate the world's infrastructure in which the customers will literally be the kings. In a world like this, contrary to the taken-for-granted situation but one which works reversely, it is aimed for the central third parties such as Facebook and Google to lose their power and the customers keep the data themselves instead of these central structures keeping the customer data. It is also envisioned that customers will be a lot more selective with regard to sharing the data that belong to them. An element that will make things more difficult for the businesses is that customers will be able to transfer from one service provider to another anytime they would like and within a few minutes. For example, a customer who receives all the banking services from a certain brand, will be able to use the service of another bank only for crypto-wallet service, transferring the whole data of his / hers. Banks will not have the chance to build a barrier to their customers so that they would not lose them. Within the envisioning of such a world, the only competitive-edge a brand will have is its provision of a smoother, seamless user experience that will require less cognitive effort compared to that of its competitors. Hence, a perfect user experience will be the most important key to gain competitive advantage for the brands. Each illusional marketing technique will be analyzed respectively in depth in the remaining parts of the book.

References

16. Pisters, Patricia. *The Neuro-Image: A Deleuzian Film-Philosophy of Digital Screen Culture.* Stanford, CA: Stanford University Press, 2012.
17. Kahn, Barbara E. *Global Brand Power: Leveraging Branding for Long-Term Growth.* Wharton Digital Press, 2013.
18. Carey, Susan. "Airlines Try Signature Fragrances, but Not Everyone Is on Board," *Wall Street Journal,* 1 Feb. 2015, https://www.wsj.com/articles/airlines-try-signature-fragrances-but-not-everyone-is-on-board-1422832562 accessed 12 May 2018
19. Csikszentmihalyi, Mihaly, & Csikszentmihalyi, Isabella S., eds. *Optimal Experience: Psychological Studies of Flow in Consciousness.* New York: Cambridge University Press, 1992.
20. Ertemel, Adnan V. "Implications of Blockchain Technology on Marketing," *Journal of International Trade, Logistics and Law, 4:*2 (2018), pp. 35-44.
21. Duhigg, Charles. *The Power of Habit: Why We Do What We Do in Life and Business.* New York: Random House, 2012.
22. Phelps, Elizabeth A. "Emotion and cognition: Insights from studies of the human amygdala," *Annu. Rev. Psychol. 57* (Jan 2006), pp. 27-53.
23. Martin, Neale, & Morich, Kyle. "Unconscious mental processes in consumer choice: Toward a new model of consumer behavior," *Journal of Brand Management,* 18:7 (2011), pp. 483-505.
24. Gladwell, Malcolm. *Outliers: The Story of Success.* New York: Little, Brown, 2008.
25. Campbell, Joseph. *The Hero with a Thousand Faces.* New York: Pantheon, 1949.
26. Christensen, Clayton M., & Raynor, Michael E. *The Innovator's Solution: Creating and Sustaining Successful Growth.* Harvard Business School Press, 2003.
27. Dixon, Chris, "Crypto Tokens: A Breakthrough in Open Network Design" *Medium,* 1 Jun 2017. https://medium.com/@cdixon/cryptotokens-a-breakthrough-in-open-network-design-e600975be2ef

PART 4

STORYTELLING

> *Human beings are social creatures - They enjoy listening, sharing, telling, exaggerating and extending. In short, they love stories ....*

As the world is getting digitized and robotized, elements that are peculiar to humans become more valuable. Amidst these developments, we now pay our *attention* to more original, more authentic, more humanistic, more genuine and more realistic contents among many that compete to get our attention. So, what is the structure of a humanistic message like?

We as human beings are social creatures. We have been living in the form of tribes this way or another since the primitive ages. We are constantly involved in an interaction with other people around us. We enjoy listening, sharing, telling, exaggerating, extending. Shortly, we love stories because we have been brought up with stories since we were born. Stories always work universally to get our attention, to make us learn a lesson and point a moral, take action and to get inspiration. Thus, we believe that life has a meaning and purpose. What's more, we identify ourselves with the heroes of the stories. In short, being humanistic, within the context in this book, requires speaking in the language of a story or narrative.

The Concept of Story

> *Story is a character-based script that explains the effort each character puts in so as to overcome difficulties towards an important target.*

Story is a character-based script that explains the effort each character puts in so as to overcome difficulties towards an important target. In stories, the hero gets the support of a source and puts up a struggle against a common enemy to be able to achieve the target.

Storytelling is the expression of the message the brand wishes to convey by benefiting from the story which has the strength to impress and influence human beings.

The Power of Stories

The human brain has been programmed to listen to stories since the creation. Powerful stories are retained in the minds of the listeners even after decades.

Brain is in the alert mode and also in the mode of questioning all the time with the survival instinct. Everything else is in a sort of competition with it. Stories, on the other hand, inspire confidence and when it comes to stories, the brain gives a break and unwinds. The questioning brain is bypassed when it believes in a story and is drawn in a flow.

Today, it is of critical importance to create stories that are worth paying attention to and sharing.

> *No matter how good the content is, only the brands that have a "good story" win in our current era amidst the abundance of products and services.*

The only way to pass the legends and holy books from generation to generation is through stories. Almost in all of the holy books, the Creator gives a message to people in the best way they will understand through stories. Knowledge and experience are shared from generation to generation by means of stories as well. The identities of the communities, the values they are supposed to assume and the limits of their behavior with their purest form are found with their concrete entity in stories. Communities also act superior to the other ones by means of their stories.

Historically, stories have always inspired communities and cultures as well as nations.

In the modern era, companies that represent brands remind us of old communities. They tell their internal and external stakeholders including their employees the values of the company, its vision and targets, along with its heroes and enemies. With its story that is authentic and finds its equivalent in the community, the company tells people who it is and what is the reason for its existence.

From the perspective of the employees, the story of a brand conveys the values that the brand does not ever make any concession no matter what happens, and also communicates how to act in tough times. The employees of today seek more than just working for the sake of earning money; rather they look for satisfaction at psychological level as well. Strong brands, which have an authentic story, have a magnetic effect in the eyes of their employees.

In the modern marketing understanding, it is essential to perceive people as individuals who have a mind, a heart and soul rather than seeing them merely as consumers who give money. In addition, people tend to listen to those who share the values they possess. In addition, they want to feel that they are part of a cause they care about. Accordingly, they support the ones that have a new discourse regarding the fundamental problems of human beings.

Storytelling, in this regard, is the first and most important step in illusional marketing strategy, and it is of critical significance for brands in the attention economy, rendering people notice and prefer the brand, and even become the advocates and defenders of the brand.

Step by Step Storytelling

Brands use storytelling for two purposes. The first one is 'storybranding' which refers to storytelling at macro level as a strong element of strategic brand positioning. Secondly, storytelling is used as an operational communication method at micro level. The ideal one is that both uses are in coordination, strengthening each other in the integrated efforts of the brand. The next section of the book will analyze both of these storytelling methods in detail.

After the brand designs its story successfully at macro level, it would be the ideal thing for the brand to implement an integrative approach by making use of stories at micro level in its communication strategy.

StoryBranding

StoryBranding which means storytelling at macro level is concerned with the fact that the brand has a story regarding humanity, and the mission, vision and values, making the entire brand communication be in harmony. In other words, StoryBranding concerns the brand at the strategic level.

Storytelling Through the Role of Equalizing the Brand Identity and Brand Image

Brand identity is a phenomenon designed by a brand based on what kind of associations the brand is supposed to evoke in the eyes of the consumers when that particular brand springs to their minds. On the other hand, brand image expresses the perception in the consumers related to the brand. Ideally, it is desired that the perceived, that is to say, the brand image and what is designed, that is to say, the brand identity to be identically the same. However, in reality, there is always a gap that occurs between the brand identity and brand image. Stories come to the stage at this point and enable the message the brand wishes to express and the brand image it wants to form to be conveyed to the other party in an effective way [28].

---

[28] Klaus Fog, *Storytelling: Branding in Practice,* Springer, 2005.

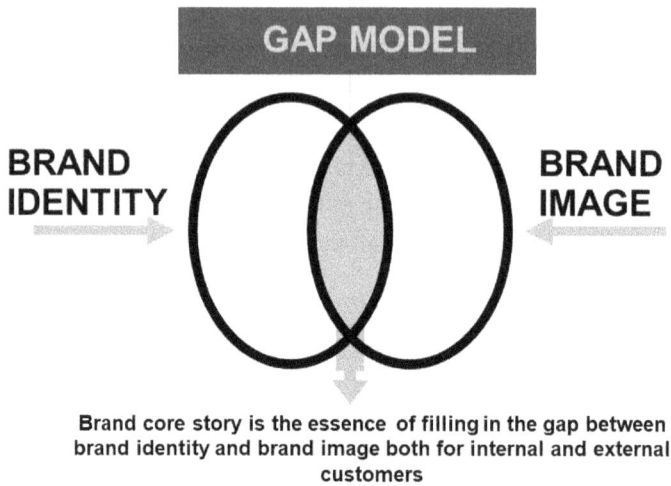

GAP MODEL

BRAND IDENTITY

BRAND IMAGE

Brand core story is the essence of filling in the gap between brand identity and brand image both for internal and external customers

Figure 4.1 Gap Model in Branding (adopted from Fog (2010))

People reflect their world views, personality and the values they uphold through symbols and by means of visual expression. Consumers do not only buy the product, but also the brand's reason for existence, the world view it represents and its culture as well. One typical example of this is that Coca-Cola is an iconic symbol of American culture. Harley Davidson brand is an example of a strong brand in that it represents the free spirit and a parallel vision of the world. Harley Davidson fans are so loyal to the brand that they even make a tattoo of the brand on their bodies.

> *The best marketing is the one that does not appear like marketing but like a story.*

In our current time, it has become meaningless to compete with the product and price. Brands are becoming distinct with authentic experiences they present to their consumers. Along with the facts, brands that are literally powerful enable consumers to experience authentic feelings and sensations they may not find elsewhere.

Godin, in the book entitled *All Marketers Tell a Story,* states that production was important in the 1950s when marketing was a secondary function, however, today the power curve has reversed. Almost every product can be produced easily and at a cheap price (considering the reality of China). Yet, the main problem is that everything produced cannot be sold easily. Godin explains that the solution to this biggest problem of marketing would be to leave aside the classical marketing strategies completely and to craft a story peculiar to the brand[29]

In another book of his, *Tribes,* Godin summarizes the power of stories in modern communities as follows: "Today, consumers no longer believe in what you say, they rarely believe in what you demonstrate. Sometimes, they happen to believe what their friends tell them. Yet, they always believe in the stories they tell themselves. Powerful brands give people stories that they will tell themselves and believe in those as well."

Storytelling as the Only Way of Becoming Differentiated

Today, consumers can easily find a cheaper version of a product with the same functions and features they are seeking. It is important to bring to the fore the benefits and utility of the product to the consumers through marketing studies. However, at the point that has been reached today, it is not possible to become differentiated through the benefits and utility presented as being peculiar to the consumer either.

Storytelling for Meaning

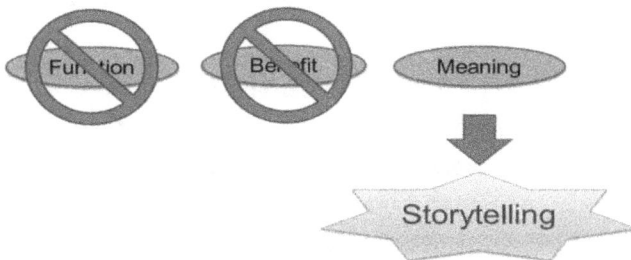

Figure 4.3 Storytelling as the only way to become differentiated

---

[29] Seth Godin, *All Marketers Are Liars: The Power of Telling Authentic Stories in a Low-Trust World,* Portfolio, 2005.

This being the case, brands become differentiated by *presenting authentic meanings to the consumers*, with the metaphysical benefit rather than the physical one, which is the only way to differentiate. For example, in the past, a washing machine commercial used to give information on facts such as the spin speed of the machine, its washing capacity and similar features. Recently, producers of white goods are trying to become differentiated by pointing out their products being of A+++ energy class, saving energy and water, and that they are a better choice for future generations. In brief, they emphasize the meaning they add to. Storytelling, with this aspect, is of critical importance for brands as the element which adds meaning.

Brand Personality and Storytelling

Brand personality is a set of human characteristics attributed to the brand, and it carries both functional and symbolic meanings.[30] In the formation of the brand personality, all the communication activities of the brand contribute to the use of the product, thus to the functional use of the brand as well as its symbolic positioning from the viewpoint of consumers.

Brand personality is an important element that influences the choice of the consumer. In promotional activities, the expressions presented to the consumer are an important factor in the formation of the brand personality.[31]

The brand is preferred by the consumers to the extent the brand personality overlaps with the personality type the consumers are interested in.

Brand personality becomes incarnated through storytelling. The hero of the story represents the vision and values of the brand. By overcoming the challenges along the way through the character type the hero portrays, the happy end is attained. And, as the consumers associate the hero of the story with the desired character they identify with themselves

---

[30] Jennifer Aaker, "Dimensions of Brand Personality," *Journal of Marketing Research* 34 (1997), pp. 342-352.

[31] Chung K. Kim, Dongchul Han, & Seung-Bae Park, "The effect of brand personality and brand identification on brand loyalty: Applying the theory of social identification," *Japanese Psychological Research* 43:4 (2001), pp. 195-206.

in their unconscious, their interest and rate of preferring the brand naturally increases. In its rip-roaring commercial series, the Apple brand implemented storytelling in a successful way. In the series, the story that the brand represents provides clashes and conflicts through the opposite values Apple owns vis-a-vis those of its rival Microsoft/ Intel based personal computer (PC), thus, the commercials convey a powerful message demonstrating why the brand is superior each time through such clashes.

Figure 4.4: Get a Macintosh or PC Commercial Series
https://youtu.be/pG43ylhODQg

The Golden Circle of Brands

Within the context of Marketing 3.0, brands come to the fore in the competitive environment to the extent that they can relate the story of the brand to the basic problems of human beings and to the extent they can craft the brand story and express it successfully.

People who have a story are always appealing. The same applies for the brands. Brands, which have a good story, are always striking and reason for preference. They are also regarded as worthy of being shared on social media. In Marketing 3.0 understanding, brands which promise a strong value are the ones that have accomplished to develop an important discourse related to human beings, their values and problems.

Simon Sinek notes the critical importance of the fact that a brand should explain why it exists in relation with the view of life and fundamental values of the consumers and the reason why consumers should choose that particular brand. Sinek explains this process with what he defines as "the golden circle"[32].

Made up of nested smaller circles, the question 'what' lies in the outer circle. Almost all brands can explain what they produce in some way or another. The circle in the middle explains the question of 'how'. Some brands explain how they influence the lives of individuals. The innermost and most significant circle explains the question of 'why'. What is important here is the reason 'why' the brand is to be preferred with respect to the lives of people, their fundamental value judgments, concerns and hopes. Very few brands provide an authentic answer to this question of 'why', a question to which people attach importance.

People don't buy what you do; they buy why you do it, namely they buy your story. -- *Simon Sinek*

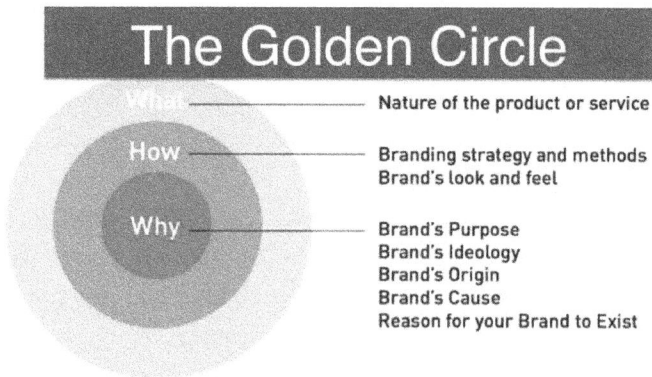

The Golden Circle

What —— Nature of the product or service

How —— Branding strategy and methods
Brand's look and feel

Why —— Brand's Purpose
Brand's Ideology
Brand's Origin
Brand's Cause
Reason for your Brand to Exist

Figure 4.5: Starting with the question 'Why' - Simon Sinek

---

[32] Simon Sinek. *Start With Why: How Great Leaders Inspire Everyone to Take Action,* Portfolio, 2009.

For example, the Apple Brand has been able to craft a story that conveys what it believes together with the entire corporation and employees, and reflects successfully onto its products with its tagline 'Think Different!', and understanding that user experience can every time be better. Starting with the iMac and Pod, and continuing with the iPhone and iPad, the brand has incarnated its story and its claim in its devices. Since Apple is able to provide the answer to the question 'Why' successfully to people and make them believe in its story, it has been able to generate a large mass of fanatics who stay wide awake and wait in queue the night before it launches a new device model that starts with the letter 'i' but one that no one knows yet what it exactly is.

> *A story has a lasting impact only if the brand has a different discourse regarding humanity.*

Figure 4.6: The story queue in front of an Apple Store

Storytelling at Micro Scale: Giving the Message through Storytelling

If the story has found its equivalence, then the consumer brain gets out of the critical mode. As the questioning and rational left-brain has been relaxed, the right brain in which emotions, feelings, pain and longing predominate intervenes. The person is in a hypnotic state during this mode. It is this powerful aspect of the stories which enables the brands to use stories for promotional purposes and also as tactical tools in communication practices.

In practices of storytelling that has been implemented successfully in many advertisements, a typical story flow is followed.

The Components of a Story

In story branding, it is also necessary to act in accordance with the story structure as a means of communication. There are four basic components that are applied in almost all the stories. These are the main message of the story, the conflict, the characters and the plot, respectively.

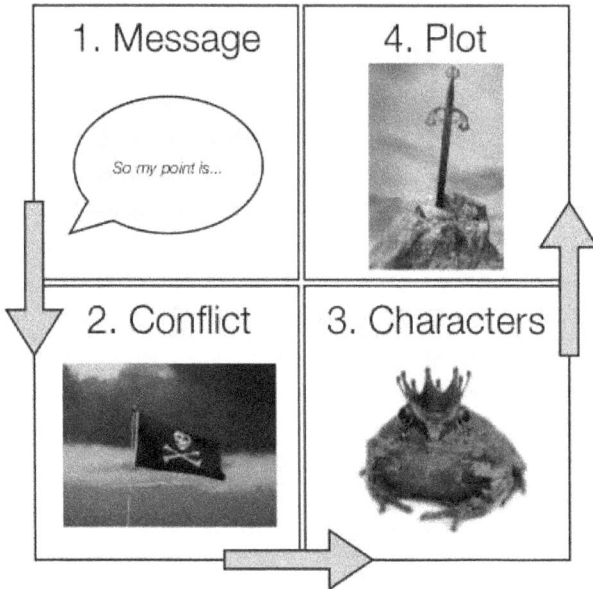

1. Message	4. Plot
So my point is...	
2. Conflict	3. Characters

Figure 4.7: Four Basic Elements of Storytelling

1. The Main Message of the Story

Imagine a story that does not have a clear message. In this situation, how successful would it be to devise a brand strategy? Unless you have a concise and clear message, there would be no point in telling a story no matter which aim you engage in. In the story named "The Rabbit and The Tortoise", this message is conveyed: "no matter how fast you are, if you do not care, you will fall behind in the race, and you will eventually lose." A story which does not have a message or morale at the end is doomed to lack appeal. The message conveyed should also be one that can enable the person to relate the story to himself / herself, and internalize it. Specifically, in the development of brand strategy, this message needs to be a single one that has been worked on very well and it also needs to be as plain and simple as possible. Such a message for the Nike brand is 'Never contend with being the second best, just do it.' For Volvo, this message is 'Safety First.' Ideally, the main message of the story needs to be in line with the 3.0 marketing rationale and should touch upon the fundamental problems of humanity with its spiritual aspect.

Just like the main message of the story being dealt with throughout the story, the entire communication strategy of the brand constantly needs to emphasize and reinforce the main commitment that the brand has expressed through narration. Within this scope, it is important to visualize the story and make all the visuals of the brand explain this message so that the story can find a long-lasting place in the minds of the consumers. For instance, the logo of the Nike brand represents a winner athlete when followed from left to right. Accordingly, the brand that gets strength from this powerful logo has started using only the logo visual without the Nike in written form.

2. The Conflict

A story in which every element is well-aligned and no conflict exists naturally tends to be very boring. So, what makes such stories that boring? The answer is hidden in the genetic code of humans. Human beings always look out for harmony. In cases when harmony and equilibrium are disrupted, humans get stressed and they take action; they struggle until the harmony and equilibrium are restored. Imagine that two of your acquaintances have a conflict on a certain issue. You try to make peace between them and you cannot feel relieved until you achieve this. There is no better way than creating a conflict situation to make people take action and involve them in a cause or get them to follow and watch the story till the end with interest. The hero of the story appears and converts the unforeseeable chaotic environment into a harmonious and organized one again.

Conflict is not a bad phenomenon in storytelling. On the contrary, the conflict situation is a unique means of telling what is right and what is wrong to the listeners from the viewpoint of the person who created the story. The conflict should neither be a total chaos that would distract the listeners nor a simple conflict situation whose solution could easily be figured out by everyone. Therefore, an optimum equilibrium is to be observed while designing the conflict.

3. Characters

Following the main message of the story and conflict, the roles of the players in the story have their turn. The hero of the story (protagonist), the other party and further elements that complement the story are chosen by making use of classical character types. The better the characters chosen are described, the easier it would be to portray the passions and capabilities of these characters. The hero of the story incarnates the brand in the universe of stories. It should also be noted that it is required to take into account whether the customers can identify themselves with this character or not while finalizing the character of the story hero. The character types and brands that set an example for each character type are presented in the table below.

Archetype	Enables people to	Brand
Creator	Make something new	Williams-Sonoma
Caregiver	Care for others	AT&T
Ruler	Take control	American Express
Jester	Have fun	Miller Lite
Regular Guy/Orphan	Be OK as themselves	Wendy's
Lover	Find and give love	Hallmark
Hero/Warrior	Be brave	Nike
Outlaw/Destroyer	Break the rules	Harley-Davidson
Magician	Bring about transformation	Calgon
Innocent	Retain or renew faith	Ivory
Explorer/Seeker	Maintain Independence	Levi's
Sage	Understand their world	Oprah
Source: Margaret Mark and Carol S. Pearson - *The Hero and The Outlaw*		

Table 3: Character Types and Well-known Heroes

Source: Mark, M.,& Pearson, C. S. (2001). *The hero and the outlaw: Building extraordinary brands through the power of archetypes*

4. Plot

The plot is the last element of the story components. With the help of the plot, the events in a story are narrated in a chronological or logical manner within a cause-and-effect relationship. The plot can be composed of either simple structures or intertwined complex ones.[33] The most commonly used model as regards the plot is the Olsson's model, also known as the Hollywood model, since it is used in Hollywood films.[34] According to this model, the story begins in a harmonious world in which its main characters are introduced first. Then, the conflict process develops. Having reached the point of no return ensuing the escalation of the conflict, events in the story and the level of tension in the story constantly escalates; and

---

[33] Wikipedia, "Plot (narrative)," accessed date 5 Feb 2020. https://en.wikipedia.org/wiki/Plot_(narrative)

[34] Ola Olsson. *Hurmanbörjarenfil. Nordiska Theater kommitten*, Helsingfors, 1982.

when the tension reaches the peak called climax, the hero of the story triumphs as a result of a surprising support. Then, the foreseeable harmony is quickly reverted and the story comes to an end.

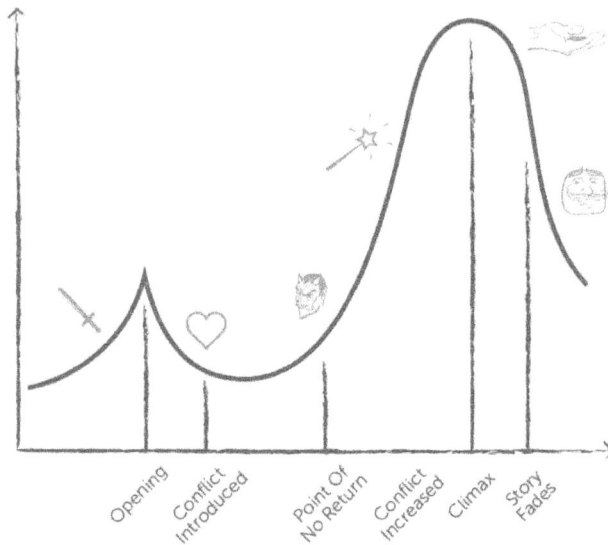

Figure 4.8 The Hollywood Model of Storytelling

The Story Model

There is more or less fiction in every story constructed.[35] The general model of stories is provided as follows.

Each story has a winner. In a story in which Prince charming saves the princess from the evil monster, the winner is the kingdom itself. The hero or the protagonist of the story gains victory as a result of the support provided to him (with the help of a magic wand) in the toughest times in a clash with the enemy for a cause. In our story, the aim is to save the kingdom and the princess. The hero of the story is prince charming. The beneficiary is also the prince himself. The enemy figure is the monster and the

---

[35] Seth Godin, *Tribes: We Need You to Lead Us,* Portfolio, 2008.

evil spirit it represents. In this context, the magic wand/ its support in the story is in fact the glory of kindness and perseverance.

When we adapt the same model to the Apple brand, we see that the hero of the story is Steve Jobs himself.

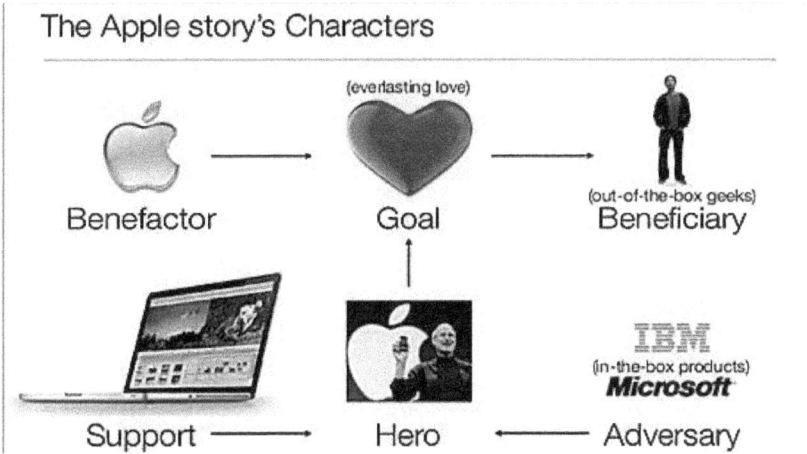

Figure 4.9: The Story Canvas: Apple Example

An experience of exceptional simplicity is the goal of the brand. The winner is the Apple brand. The beneficiaries are extraordinarily productive consumers who see themselves different. In this story, the magic wand is the extraordinary product of the brand. The hero of the story is the visionary founder Steve Jobs himself. The adversary figure refers to rival companies such as Microsoft and IBM.

Let's apply the same model to the Nike brand. In the particular case of Nike, the winner is again the brand itself. The goal is the winning mentality. The beneficiaries are the end consumers who want to be like athletes. The magic wand (that is to say support) is the courage needed to be able to proceed and get ahead overcoming the barriers. The hero of the story is the visionary founders of the brand. The adversary is the mentality of making do with the second best. Note that, in stories, the adversary figure does not always have to take shape in flesh and bones, but it can also represent a certain mentality.

Suggestions for Creating a Brand Story

- *Your story must have a hero. This is usually the brand itself. Have your target audience relate themselves to the hero of the story.*

- *Tell your story to your target audience with passion and ensure that your main message matches the brand image and brand identity.*

- *Visualize your story while telling your brand story. It is easier for consumers to remember the visual images.*

- *After you have started to publish your brand story online, interact with your audience and help your new stories be developed.*

- *After you have given a name to your brand story, by using the hashtag with the story, launch campaigns via social media (as in the example of #AlwaysLikeAGirl).*

> *As can be seen in the film industry in its simplest form, people follow stories that overlap with their own values, concerns and interests till the end as if they were hypnotized, and also share the ones they like with their social circle.*

INTERVIEW: Sinan Sülün, Storyteller, Founder of StoryZone

How does the story of Sinan Sülün start and how does it develop?

"Man resembles the place he lives in" says Edip Cansever in a poem of his. "Resembles its water, its soil, the fish swimming in the sea, the flower pushing its soil…" I, too, looked like the places I have lived in just like everyone else. This country, Istanbul, the house I live in, the people I have met, the dreams I have had as well as the storytellers I have met.

I was born in Istanbul in 1980. In 1997, I got into the Department of Economics at Istanbul University. It wasn't a conscious choice of mine, but an arbitrary disposition of the counseling instructor. "Go for Economics", the instructor told me, "If you become a banker, you'll get paid well". So I followed this advice. And yet, I never really liked it. I didn't have an issue with numbers, yet I didn't want to turn into one of those people who constantly work with and engage in numbers. Goethe says, "Man knows himself only in man." That is true. I got to know myself through the dreamers I met at Istanbul University and the authors I read at the time. It was only then I decided to become a journalist so as to write and tell people's stories. While I was doing my master's degree in the Department of Communication Studies at Marmara University, I started to work for culture and art magazines.

However, when the magazines I worked for stopped being published due to the economic crisis, I entered corporate life. I preferred jobs through which I could both make money and also collect stories. I worked as a representative in the pharmaceutical industry in the field of cancer for four years. It was a tough period in terms of its human aspect, but it was really a precious time for me as a storyteller. In this period, I published the story book *Karahindiba* (which can be translated into English as *Dandelion*). After a while, I changed my division and started working as a trainer in the training department of the company. I started writing my second book while doing the training there. My second book, *Kırlangıç Dönümü* (which can be translated into English as *The Swallow Season*), takes its beginning from these years and its end from the time when I left corporate life.

Long story short, I quit corporate life in 2014, and started working for training companies individually on a freelance basis. In the period when I was doing the training work, storytelling was a discipline that I was particularly interested in. As a man of letters who knows the power of art and as a white collar who is familiar with the needs of corporate life, I have merged these two fields. Afterwards, I have created my own models of training by studying, attending training programs on the relevant issues, working and thinking. Nowadays, I still continue to offer training at Dinamo Consulting as a "storyteller" and also consultancy services for various companies.

What do you think is the most fundamental element of storytelling?

There are many essential elements of storytelling. The subject that I mostly focus on during the training or consultations I offer is the "meaning" created by the story, its being memorable and the value it creates on persuasion.

In order for a message to be memorable and persuasive, the message needs to be delivered through storytelling. Because figures, graphics and messages presented merely via informative words without any emotions -however well-explained they may be- cannot be memorable or persuasive. In order for something to affect us, it must first touch our feelings. If and only if things manage to touch our emotions, then they can have a lasting effect on us.

Robert McKee says, "Our mind has a language of stories, and if a person presents his/her own thoughts through stories, the other person, i.e., the listener will not resist that idea. On the contrary, that person will embrace the narration." This underlying essence of this notion is based on the fact that the brain works with visuals.

This is because the act we call communication is, in fact, the exchanging of pictures. While creating a brand story, selling a product or trying to persuade people, we try to create the same image that forms in our minds in the minds of those who are listening to us as well. The best way to create this image is possible through describing the idea, service and brand through storytelling and narration.

Scientific studies show that the rate of recalling a piece of information that has been delivered in written format or verbally is 10% following a period of 72 hours. However, when we present the same piece of information through visualization, then this recalling rate increases up to 65%. That's where storytelling comes in. Storytelling enwraps the information delivered with metaphors, descriptions and emotive words, thus provides the person who is listening, a picture that he / she will not be able to forget. Only then we will be able to turn into people who look at the same picture, have the same feelings and share the same dream/target.

And of course the greatest power of the story comes from "the meaning it creates". " We are currently living in the "Conceptual Age" as Daniel Pink put it. From our purchasing choices to performance interviews, to job interviews and marketing strategies, we are constantly in pursuit of meaning everywhere. Concepts such as "features and benefits" are no longer as meaningful to us as they used to be.

The abundance era created by the 20th century has dedifferentiated (similarized) products, services and brands. As of the 21st century, the only thing that can break down this differentiation and make a difference lies in the meaning we create. Hence, when we used to buy a new washing machine, we would simply look at its technical features and benefits in the past, but now, we look to the future that is compatible with the nature it will create for our children, and one that would run on less energy and water.

While the benefits a brand created for us were of importance in the past, now we tend to value the meaning that it creates for us. Today, we listen to and accept the one that appeals to our feelings, rather than the one that addresses our mind. In other words, every product we buy, every brand we are committed to and every institution we work with eagerness has a story. These stories connect us to these products, brands and institutions with invisible threads and affect the decisions we make. And we are able to present the reality solely through story-telling, touching emotions and creating an image. As can be seen in Forster's well-known observation, the reality is "the king and the queen are dead", but the story is that "The queen died and the king died from his grief."

Looking at the big picture, can you share with us the place of storytelling, how it should be implemented and the future projections of business managers with respect to brand management?

There is something that I frequently share in training and consultations, that is, you must first believe in your story yourself in order to become a good storyteller. If we do not have belief in the story of our brand, our product or ourselves, then no matter how many times we explain this and how hard we may try, it cannot really be conveyed to others. Those who listen to us can see that we speak very well, that our advertisement is highly impressive and our idea is pretty innovative. Yet, they can also sense that we don't actually believe in what we're saying. One believes in what he sees through the heart, that is, what he feels, not in what he sees through the human eye. Turgut Uyar says "There is always something that's left behind". What remains of our brand is directly proportional to our belief in the story we tell.

If we simply have faith, the rest is technical and easy. There are several techniques for storytelling. Brand managers can use these techniques for both their brands and their leadership. In addition, these techniques can be learned, developed and applied in business life, the related results can also be obtained quickly.

Can you also touch upon a couple of examples of national and/or international success stories?

110

I think we are quite successful in creating brand stories nationally, particularly in the advertising sector. However, we do not use storytelling that often in business life while we are delivering presentations, creating a marketing strategy or motivating and inspiring our team as a leader. We generally use a language that is framed by didactic and informative words that are delivered from the top to the bottom. There are many companies which have been trying to improve the competency of their employees in this regard for the last few years. These are companies which can envision the future better and feel the future, attaching importance to the generational differences and acting accordingly. In this sense, it looks promising.

There are numerous successful examples in the international arena. One of these stories that has so far had the biggest effect on me is the story of Xerox. Upon realizing that the technical staff had learned to repair the machines by telling each other the stories they had gone through, rather than reading about technical details from manuals, Xerox compiled these business stories in a database named Eureka. Thus, people began to learn how to repair a machine and how to cope with that difficulty through the stories of another individual. Fortune estimates that this project is worth $100 million for the company.

Some strategies that brands use for differentiation in storytelling are as follows:

- Identifying and embracing the aspect that brand renders unique in competition, and building its entire strategy on this. This is the only way to ensure a sustainable competitive advantage. Sustaining a competitive advantage may be possible by highlighting a feature that competitors cannot mimic despite their efforts.

- Brands tend to adopt a color and use it continuously so as to realize differentiation in competition.

- The principal goal of brands in storytelling is to evoke emotions in the customers selected. For this, it is critical to design messages that capture consumers' hearts, and that are in line with their cultural norms as well as value judgments, making them say "Yeah, that's me!"

> *In a highly competitive environment, consumers pay attention to brands that view them as human beings and not just as customers (Marketing 3.0) and that have a different and interesting discourse on humanity, namely brands that have a story.*

References

28. Fog, Klaus. *Storytelling: Branding in Practice.* New York: Springer, 2005.

29. Godin, Seth. *All Marketers Are Liars: The Power Of Telling Authentic Stories In A Low-Trust World.* New York: Portfolio, 2005.

30. Aaker, Jennifer. "Dimensions of Brand Personality," *Journal of Marketing Research*, 34 (1997), pp. 342-352.

31. Kim, K. Chung, Dongchul Han & Seung-Bae Park. "The effect of brand personality and brand identification on brand loyalty: Applying the theory of social identification, "*Japanese Psychological Research* 43:4 (2001), pp. 195-206.

32 Sinek, Simon. *Start With Why: How Great Leaders Inspire Everyone To Take Action.* Portfolio, 2009.

33. Wikipedia. "Plot (narrative)." Accessed 5 Feb 2020. https://en.wikipedia.org/wiki/Plot_(narrative)

34. Olsson, Ola. *Hurmanbörjarenfil. Nordiska Teater kommitten*, Helsingfors, 1982.

35. Godin, Seth. *Tribes: We Need You To Lead Us.* New York: Portfolio, 2008.

PART 5

User Experience

Storytelling is the first and most important stage of illusional marketing. This stage is followed by user experience and gamification, respectively.

The first recent view on the concept of user experience appears as *User's Experience* in the book *User Centered System Design: New Perspectives on Human-Computer Interaction* written by Donald Norman and Stephen Draper in 1986. Donald Norman, regarded as the father of user experience concept, is one of the founders of Nielsen Norman Group according to which user experience is the total sum of the positive and negative experiences that occur as a result of the users' interactions with the brands and their products.[36] This experience encompasses all interactions with the brand on any platform or media, which is a matter that is very often overlooked. For example, many e-commerce sites regard the user experience merely as the interactions occurring on the digital medium. Therefore, they do not attach importance to the users' experiences on offline aspects like delivery and after sales services Yet, applications that cause customers to have bad experiences on offline media and make them cross or resented lead the interaction with the brand to come to an ultimate end.

On the contrary, the sort of user experience that pleases the customers by surprising them on the offline environments increases customer satisfaction, and as a consequence, their loyalty as well.

---

[36] Don Norman and Jacob Nielsen, "The Definition of User Experience," Nielsen Norman Group, accessed 23 Sept 2016. https://www.nngroup.com/articles/definition-user-experience/

Figure 5.1: User Experience is a Whole

Why Does User Experience Matter?

User experience has become a critical element for the brands that have gained prominence in the recent period to come to the fore in their competition. This situation is depicted clearly in the graph provided below. As can be seen from the graph, the major user experience centric brands that are traded on the US stock markets have become more valuable by 228 % in a ten-year period vis-a-vis their competitors.

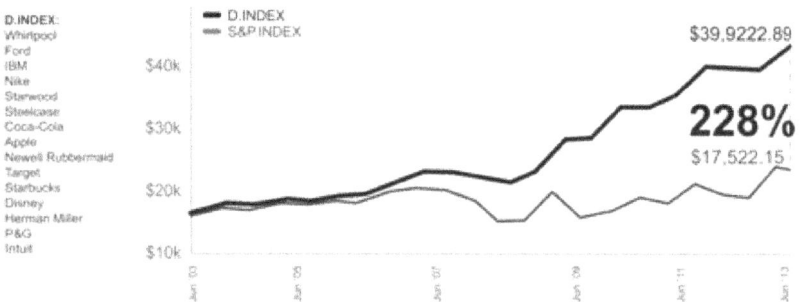

Figure 5.2: Comparison of the stock performance of user experience centric companies in the US with that of other companies

The Stages of User Experience

Norman explains user experience in a few steps including the first stage which has the sine qua non characteristics up until the ultimate desirable stage. Let now us analyze these stages respectively:

1. Meeting the Customer Need Entirely and Effortlessly

The first requirement of user experience is to fulfill all the needs of the customer in an undisputed and effortless way. A user experience that is acceptable at basic level refers to the capability of the customer as to doing what he / she wants to do in an easy way and without putting in physical and mental effort.

2. Simple and Elegant Design

In the second stage of user experience we see simplicity and elegance, which provide pleasure in its own terms and make up products which are enjoyable to use.

> *Simplicity is the ultimate sophistication. --* ***Leonardo Da Vinci***

John Maeda's book entitled *The Laws of Simplicity*[37] which is concerned with simplicity in design is a very good reference in this matter.

Figure 5.3: Simplicity as the Ultimate Sophistication: iPhone

We can provide the products of Apple as an example of simplicity in user experience. Its revolutionary approach regarding the single button

---

[37] John Maeda, *The Laws of Simplicity,* MIT Press, 2006.

that helps one do all the tasks with that button instead of resorting to a keypad has been a breakthrough in user experience with respect to smart phones. The strategy of this brand, which was initially criticized with remarks like 'it doesn't even have a keypad.', has been followed by all the competitors in time. The brand also adopts the same line in its other devices such as Apple TV.

Figure 5.4: Simplicity as the Ultimate Sophistication: Apple TV

Design Thinking Sometimes Requires to be Assertive

Design thinking during the process of designing user experience sometimes requires making very bold decisions in matters that touch human life. The Atomic clock feature of Apple can be provided as a different example regarding this matter. Having made a radical design decision, the brand decided to enable automatic time setting for day and hour based on the geographical location of the smartphone users. Although it is technically difficult to go along with this feature (due to changes in summer hour settings in each country), they defended the idea that ideal experience is one that would not cause mental exhaustion in human life. Such details might seem to be subtle and unimportant but, in the end, they have added value to human life in society.

3. Inspiring Design

The third stage, indicating literal customer satisfaction, offers an experience that goes beyond providing customers with what they want or with a list of features. Through its visual aspects, it inspires with its simple design that is far away from complexity. It also enables the customer to focus merely on what he / she wants to do.

Norman states that user experience that possesses a high quality can be obtained through a unique integration and cooperation of many different disciplines such as engineering, marketing, industrial design and interface design in the brand's products and services.

The Flow Theory

The stage at which customers focus only on what they want to do, and do not have to exert any mental effort on how they use the product or bother about which part is in which place is the peak point that is desired in user experience. Csikszentmihalyi, in the 'flow' theory he developed, explains this stage as the ultimate flow state. This stage at which a skier or a user who uses word processors on her computer or an office program to prepare a presentation focuses just on the task that she is currently engaged in, besides this, the person does not even realize how the time passed. This is the stage most desirable one and it yields the highest level of efficiency. A user experience designer is supposed to target this flow state as the ultimate state in designs.

Regarding the design of the products in line with the intuitive use, Norman's book entitled *Design of Everyday Things* is an important source for reference[38]. User experience in its best form can be realized only by a cooperation of different disciplines working together in harmony.

---

[38] Donald A. Norman, *The Design of Everyday Things: Revised and Expanded Edition,* Basic Books, 2013.

Disciplines that must be drawn on for the best user experience are provided below:

Table 4: The Dimensions of a Good User Experience

Includes useful product / service / knowledge	Benefit and Marketing
It does not have any technical errors and can be opened within a reasonable amount of time. It works on diverse platforms.	Functional, Error-free Software
It is learned easily when one wants to see the task at hand, it is remembered easily as well in a new entry.	Usability
It involves information and elements that the visitor needs and he / she turns this need into purchasing.	Convincing Design, Psychology
It is interesting, motivating, inspiring and reliable.	Visual design, graphic elements

How is User Design Formed?

Making designs favorable for the subconscious that do not make the user think is possible through products and services with high usability, which is one of the most important aspects of user experience design. Components that enhance the utility of a product or service design are learnability, efficiency, memorability and satisfaction. These components are not only the design elements of the product but they also have a positive impact with regard to its marketing.

Design That Doesn't Make You Think

We have already mentioned that an ideal user experience is one that is simple and inspiring apart from realizing what the customers want to perform. User experience design, a relatively recent discovery, aims at enabling customers to use the products intuitively without exerting any effort other than what they are already used to. It is for this very reason that this notion has been gaining more importance in the realm of marketing. More simple and plain applications have emerged accordingly over time. This notion, with its tagline design that doesn't make you think, is adopted as the basic principle in real life and the digital world.

Steve Krug has been writing on the subject matter since the very first years of the Internet[39]. He summarizes the user experience on digital media as "Don't make me think."

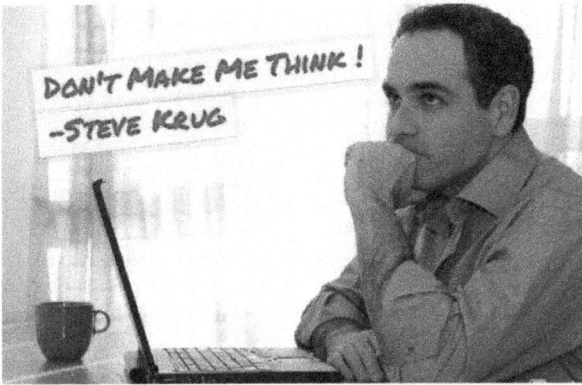

Figure- 5.5: The Slogan of User Experience: "Don't Make Me Think"

This discourse is not only used in digital media but also in real life to define ideal user experience design.

Design That Doesn't Make You Think in Real Life

There are user experiences that are in need of being developed in our daily lives that we do not notice, and yet such experiences steal a few seconds from our valuable and limited time. For instance, we all think if we have to push or pull the gate of a shopping mall just as we are going into it.

---

[39] Steve Krug, *Don't Make Me Think!: A Common Sense Approach to Web Usability*, Pearson Education, 2000.

Figure 5.6: A Door Design that Exhausts the Brain

Then, we look for the instruction "push or pull" on the door. After we see that notice, we make our decision and either pull the door or push it. The unpleasant side of this is that we have been to that shopping mall hundreds of times before. Yet, we have to exert this mental effort again and again every time we go there. This detains us from the tasks that we have to focus on in our daily lives, and when they build up, they cost us a considerable amount of time. Some experiences that steal our time are minor, on the other hand, some are really significant.

A good experience design targets a smooth experience that does not preoccupy and exhaust the brain with such secondary matters. It is not necessary to reinvent the wheel for the door example. The solution that does not require a technological mechanism and that has been implemented for many years in a lot of countries abroad is as shown in the figure. A door which does not have a handle when you have to push it to open and on the other side, which needs to be pulled, there is a handle. It is essential that the same mechanism be applied for almost all the doors not only in a building, but also for the doors in a city or a country so that the subconscious can feel relieved concerning this. If there are generally accepted rules and conventions regarding one matter, the brain is relieved and it knows how to act in an automatic pilot mode without having to exert mental effort.

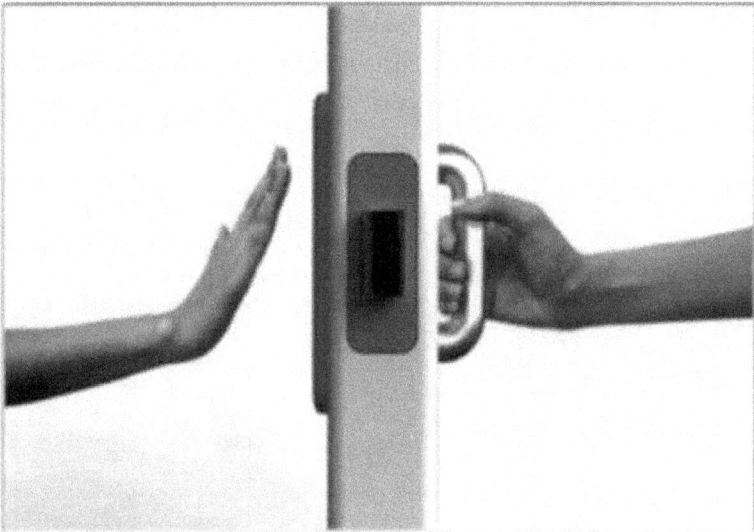

Figure 5.8: A Door Design that does not Make one Think at all

New norms are being formed regarding web-based internet experience despite being slow. Within this scope, 'responsive design' involves some invisible rules like this: on an internet site, the logo of the website is on the upper left-hand and when one navigates to any page below, she returns back to the main page whenever she clicks the logo. Since mobile platforms are relatively newer, norms that are specifically applicable for the mobile media are not that established. While looking at a visual, a finger swipe towards the upper left dimension means that the visual will disappear. This is one of the conventional mobile rules that has recently been accepted and acknowledged by everyone.

In this section of the book, you may find some inspiring examples regarding designs that don't make you think.

Design that "Doesn't Make You Think" in Fast-Moving Consumer Goods

For some of the fast-moving consumer goods consumed frequently on Amazon website, there is a feature of automatically adding the product into the shopping cart of the user in order to spare the user from the trouble of entering the site and purchasing the product when he / she runs out of it. Through this feature, which makes the user to become a subscriber of the product, the user selects a particular time period and automatic purchasing in the desired amounts is performed on behalf of the user!

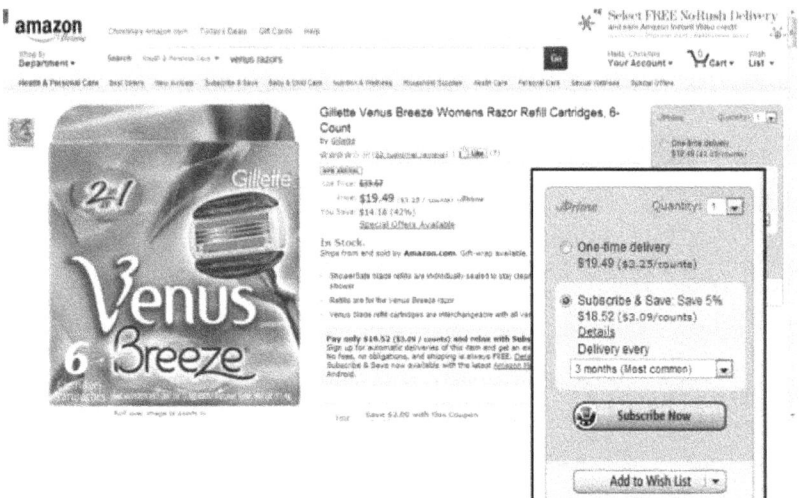

Figure 5.9: Let's Zoom it in a little bit more-
Subscription to the Product on Amazon.com

A different example by Amazon.com for fast-moving consumer goods design that doesn't make you think is the Amazon Dash button. This smart button offers an 'Internet of Things' solution since it enables automatic ordering of selected detergent brands of the user's choice when the relevant button (placed in front of devices such as a washing machine and a dishwasher) is pushed.

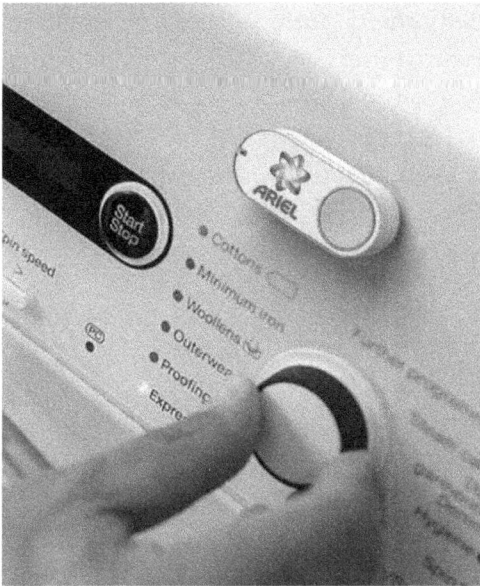

Figure 5.10: A Design that doesn't Make You Think which is realized by The Internet of Things: Amazon Dash Button

Similarly, the Birchbox website that sells socks and similar products on the internet works on a subscription basis and there is a business model inherent in this site which enables the delivery of the desired number of socks each month to your address. This saves you from the trouble of having to buy new pairs of socks again and again.

A Different App for Each Task

Another aspect of designs that don't make you think is that rather than cramming many features into one single product, such designs provide a separate solution for each task that the consumers want to do in their mind. When smart phone applications are evaluated on the basis of this rationale, it would be the most appropriate approach to have a separate mobile application (App) for each task to be performed. Facebook example could be provided for this since Facebook used to enable messaging within the Facebook application on the mobile platform in the past. Yet, afterwards, it started to offer messaging service by means of a different application, namely Messenger App. In similar fashion, on Linkedin, which is an integrative platform for professionals, a different App is being developed for every task that users want to perform in their minds. Apart from the Linkedin application that we know, it provides approximately ten different mobile apps for those who have the following different aims: to look for a job, find and learn about coworkers who work in the same corporation and fulfill certain criteria, to message in Linkedin groups and to manage the applications to the for employers' posts.

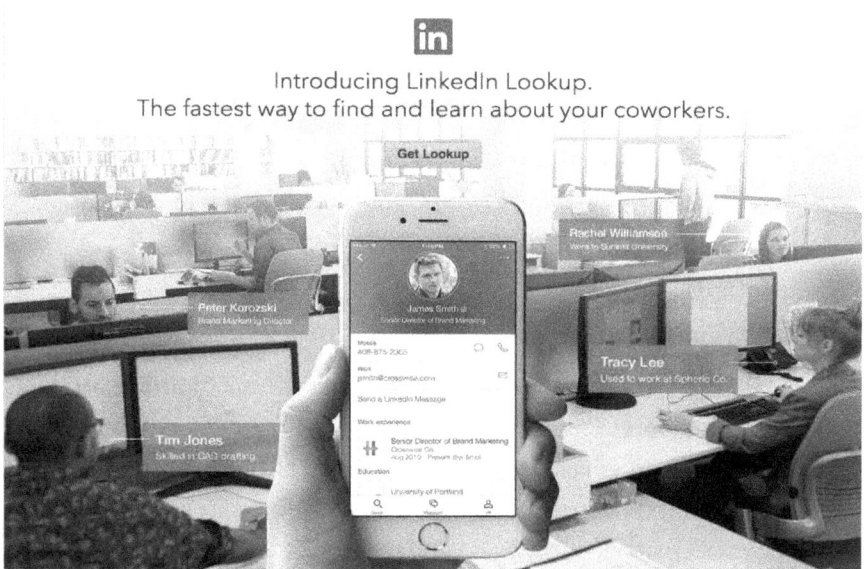

Figure 5.11: Linkedin Lookup Application to Find and Learn about Internal Coworkers

Good Examples: Design that doesn't Make You Think

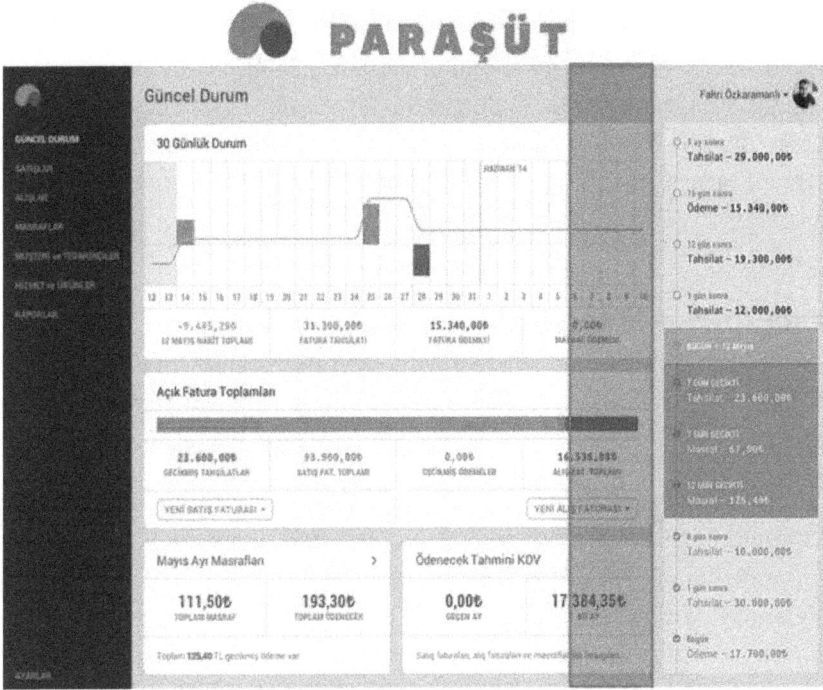

Figure 5.12: The Design of Parasut.com that Appeals to
the Unconscious and Habits

Developed by an idealist approach and with pay as you go method, Parasut.com is a cloud-based financial management solution (SaaS) whose founders have in-depth knowledge regarding user experience design. The target audience of the brand is self-employed small firm owners. The selection of all the details including the accounting jargon, the font type selected for the visuals, font size and contrast with the background has been made down to the last detail.

In the experience design, when you click any main function that lies on the menu on the left and when a vertical section of the elements that appear on the main panel is taken, a different interval width (made up of a rectangle, space, or rectangles) has been used based on which function is in use. Following a couple of months, those who have used the software encoded into their subconscious the relevant function and background components, and start assigning what appears on the menu without even looking at the name of the function. This amazing capability of the human brain reveals how immense and open-ended the notion of user experience design is. This extreme example provided for user experience design very clearly demonstrates that user experience is closely interwoven with different areas including visual design, interaction design as well as psychology.

User Experience and Gamification, Why Now?

In this section, the reason why user experience and gamification are important and why they have gained more significance today will be examined.

The significance of user experience and gamification has increased at the ultimate stage digitalization has reached. Consumers are increasingly complaining about the fact that they cannot make time for anything duly amidst the increasing amount of information and messages coming from various sources in almost every place possible. While there are many competitors that try to attract the attention of consumers, the biggest problem of brands is to attract the attention and interest people and direct this attention to themselves. The notion of attention economy is felt more starkly in the Internet of Things vision. It is at this very point that a smooth user experience design that does not exhaust the mind and one that would not require the conscious attention of the user during interaction with the brand is the most desired one.

Consumers are now in a position to spend active mental effort for almost anything they come across. This being the case, products and applications that are used intuitively enable the relaxing of the brain and thus they increasingly become a significant reason of preference.

If there are still small barriers that need to be overcome despite a user experience that has been designed in an ideal way and optimized accordingly, the product setup is gamified to lead consumers to take action in the desired manner and ensure their motivation.

A gamification expert, Michael Wu states that the only way to be able to cope with the massive amount of constantly flowing information in the Internet of Things world is gamification. There is a need for structures that tell us which signifier we must pay attention to and to carry what thing to which level, and most importantly structures that motivates us. As such, these structures are simplified with the signifiers designed in the form of a dashboard by using all the data in the relevant digital media that have to do with all aspects of our lives. In short, with the advent of the Internet of Things, the game is starting right now.

Increasing the Value Offered to the Customer through Gamification and User Experience

Now, let us examine how the value that is offered by illusional marketing techniques can be improved. There are two ways to increase the perceived value. The first one is to increase the value offered and the second one is to reduce the cost. Five dimensions in marketing are in question when the subject matter of increasing the value offered is examined. These dimensions are functional value, social value, emotional value, epistemic value and conditional value.[40]

---

[40] Jagdish N. Seth, Bruce I. Newman, & Barbara L. Gross. *Consumption Values and Market Choices: Theory and Application,* South-Western, 1991.

Dimensions of Value in Marketing and Illusional Marketing

FUNCTIONAL	SOCIAL	EMOTIONAL	EPISTEMIC	CONDITIONAL
· Performance · Specific Outcomes	· Status/ Image · Symbols	· Affective · Passion	· Entertaining · Arousing Curiosity	· Physical context · Social context

Storytelling	Gamification	Marketing 3.0

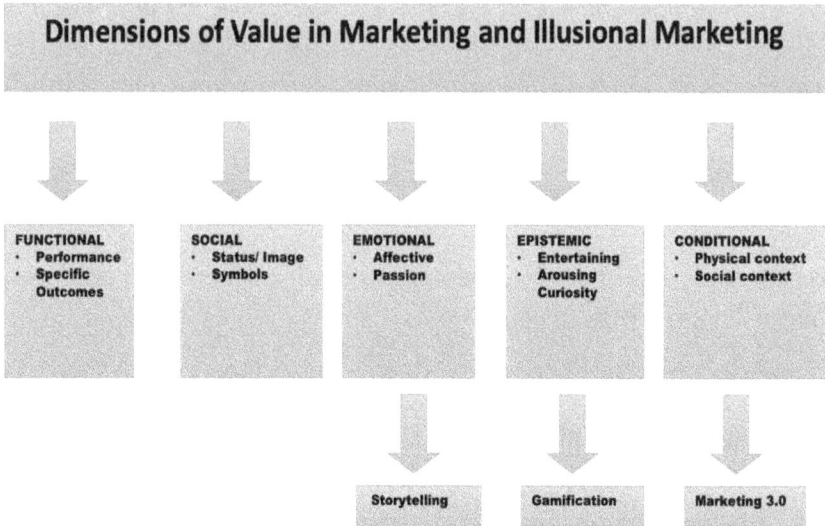

Figure 5.13: The Dimensions of Value in Marketing and Illusional Marketing

Functional value stems from the measurable dimensions related to the specific product attributes and this value demonstrates the performance of the brand's products. Engine speed and maximum speed of an automobile can be examples of functional value. The second dimension, namely social value, relates to the social status and image that could be attained through the use of the brand and its products. Emotional value refers to the benefit offered by the brand as a result of arousing feelings that will leave an impression and impact on the consumer. In other words, emotional value is the product's ability to elicit feelings and emotional stages which are influential. Through storytelling, increasing the emotional value is intended. Epistemic (novelty) value is a measure of the brand and its products with regard to arousing curiosity, bringing a novelty in the consumers' lives and triggering the desire to know about the product. Epistemic value is enhanced by gamification. Finally, conditional value takes into consideration the fact that the consumer makes his / her choice depending on his / her particular socio-cultural context and the social utility that would be provided through the use of the brand. Marketing 3.0 approach, in which activities sensitive to the environment and humanity

128

come to the fore for a more sustainable world, intends to increase the conditional value.

The second dimension in the value-based marketing approach is the cost dimension perceived by the customers. The value perceived by customers is formalized as the difference between the perceived benefit and the cost incurred. In this formula, the cost incurred is minimized so that the value can be maximized. Even if the benefit part remains the same, the perceived value increases as the cost incurred is reduced.

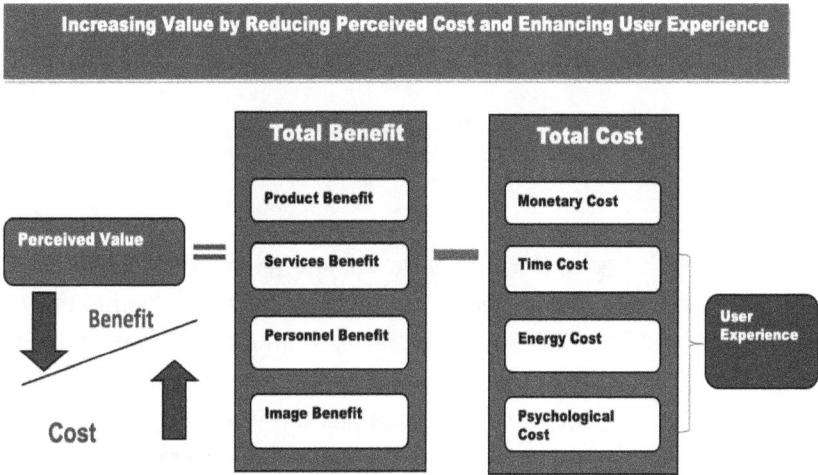

Figure 5.14: Increasing Value by Reducing the Perceived Cost and Developing the User Experience (adapted from Kotler (2000)[41]

The components of cost dimension are monetary cost, time cost, physical effort cost and mental (psychological) effort cost. A very good user experience design enables the product to be used intuitively by the consumer without any requirement of putting in mental effort, thus such an experience would allow the value to be maximized.

We can see this situation clearly in the model of Jashua Porter in which he explains designing as regards utility (usability) and motivation.

---

[41] Philip Kotler, "Marketing Management: The Millennium Edition," *Marketing Management*, 23:6 (2000), pp. 188-193.

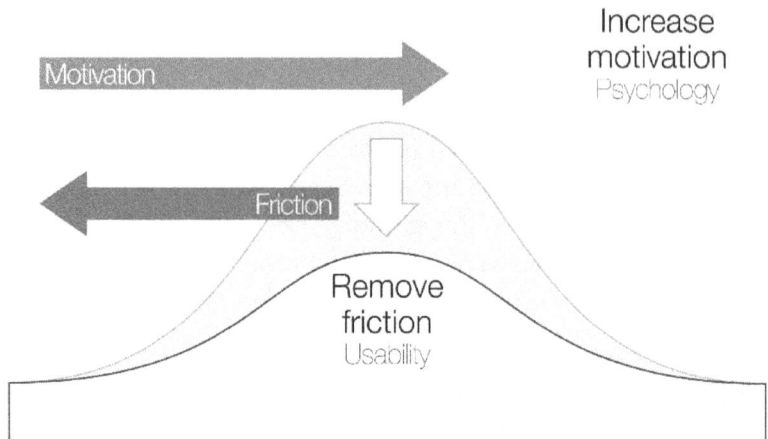

Figure 5.15: Jashua Porter, Designing with Usability and Motivation

In Porter's terms, the friction refers to anything that may prevent a user from doing the task he wants to complete. Usability, within this context, aims to eliminate any sort of obstacle, including visual, mental and so on, which would impede the user. Motivation, which happens to be the other power in the equation, encompasses the psychological techniques that encourage the user to take action. If a user is highly motivated to do a task, he may complete the task even if there are some problems on the usability dimension. In contrast, someone who lacks the motivation to do a task may quit performing the task whenever he confronts an impediment even if it is a minor one. While gamification could be a key to be utilized in order to boost motivation, the way to increase usability is to come up with a smooth and intuitive user experience design.

The Socio-Demographic Reasons for User Experience and Gamification

There are certain socio-demographic reasons why user experience and gamification have gained significance. Now, let us have a look at these justifications.

Large Masses Replace Corporate Customers

While corporate consumers used to be the typical customer of digital products in the past, this equilibrium has shifted towards individual consumers in today's world. In the past, the use of computers was intended merely for companies. Personal computers (PCs) were unimaginable up until the 1980s. Following that period, some software started to be developed gradually for personal use. Nevertheless, the complicated interfaces that corporate customers used continued to be utilized by the individual users without any stated need for simplification. We can give the graphical user interface of the applications throughout the 1990s and early 2000s as an example of this case. The typical action we used to do was to open the help menu since we did not know where to find which thing once we set up our personal computer for the first time.

Today, interaction with computers started to be performed mainly via smartphones. In addition, the masses that interact with computers are not the corporate customers of the past, and unlike the customers, who can cope with complicated interfaces although they are not as complicated as those in the past, the large masses are at stake and we may call them the average customer... While designing the user experience of the digital products, it is important to take into consideration the fact that among the users, there will also be two-year-old kids who do not know how to read and write yet, and make the designs accordingly. My daughter, who is two and a half years old, does not know how to speak properly let alone knowing how to read. However, when you give the YouTube Mobile application to her and ask her to find a song by saying the name of the song, she manages to find that song and open it in a way, which I cannot exactly figure out. The intuitive use as the slogan of user experience suggests, namely design that doesn't make you think, refers to this experience indeed. Therefore, unlike the typical Windows application of the 1990s upon whose first use we tended to open the help menu, we can use any application on AppStore or GooglePlay intuitively without having to look up the help menu. In short, it has become a necessity to design a smooth user experience so as to address the large masses.

Generation Y Has a Say

Generation Y generally refers to the generation of people who were born in the period during the early 1980s and mid-1990s. Generation Y kids grew up playing video games. This generation is the main reason why new approaches have emerged in almost all fields such as education, technology, media as well as business life. Generation Y has already started to have a voice in the workforce market[42]. Besides being more familiar with the digital technologies compared to the previous generations, the interaction techniques that used to work for earlier generations, are not effective for Generation Y. Game-like mechanisms that resemble the video games they are addicted to help this generation be more motivated in business life, education and in many other areas of real life. One of the most important reasons why gamification has become so popular today is these demographic changes. Of course, newer generations have much more acquaintance with games and technological devices.

---

[42] Richard Fry, "Millennials are the largest generation in the U.S. labor force," accessed 15 May 2018. http://www.pewresearch.org/fact-tank/2015/05/11/millennials-surpass-gen-xers-as-the-largest-generation-in-u-s-labor-force/

Good Examples to Ideal User Experience Design

The Fusion of the Real World and Virtual World:

The video of the Adobe company concerning the interaction with its products in the future provides an impressive explanation as to the naturalness the human acts in real life will be realized in the human-computer interaction as well.

Figure 5.16: A Section of Adobe's Future Applications (Video)
https://youtu.be/b0srFWU0nwM

A striking example of experience design that takes into consideration the characteristics and abilities of the target audience is the telephone user manual prepared by Samsung that addresses the elderly telephone users. A study was conducted that focused on elderly people who had difficulty in inserting the SIM card and performing the necessary steps to do the basic settings. The users can proceed step by step first by installing the telephone embedded in the user manual which was designed in the form of a book bind. By following the simple instructions indicated in the arrows of the opening pages, the users can insert the SIM card into their phone easily without experiencing any trouble.

Figure 5.17: Samsung - The Best User's Manual
https://youtu.be/ySY_W0Zpo0M

✓ Google's Project Soli

Google's project named Soli code aims at making a breakthrough in human-computer interaction. It works with radar technology that renders touching on the screen unnecessary. The company has managed to embed a very powerful radar into a very small chip, and this radar is capable of tracking the dynamic gestures of hand and finger constantly and it is able to recognize 10.000 gestures per second. With this technology, it is possible to give the required command to the relevant application upon performing the natural finger gestures we are used to doing on musical instruments without having to touch a device at all.

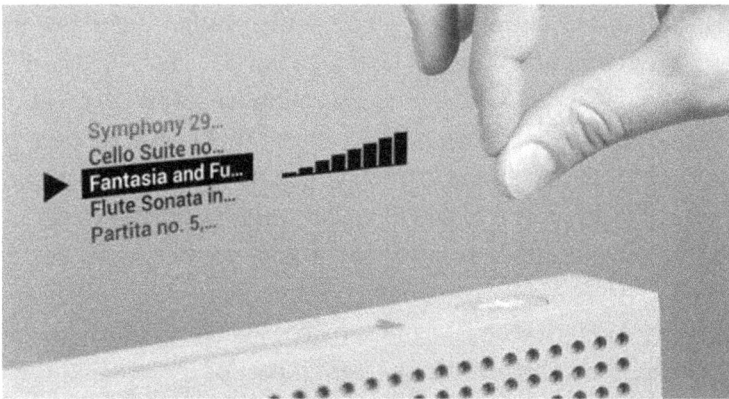

Figure 5.19: Google's Project Soli

https://www.youtube.com/watch?v=GNLiPQpjUmE

INTERVIEW: Fahri Özkaramanlı, the Co-founder of Parasut.com and Designer

Thank you very much for accepting our interview invitation and the contribution you have provided for the book. First of all, who is Fahri Özkaramanlı and what is the story of Parasut.com? We would like to hear your success story and current figures from you.

Hello, I would also like to thank you for giving a place to me in your book. I am a visual communication designer who lives in Istanbul. I believe that design has a critical importance as regards the people's relationship with technology in their daily lives. Accordingly, I have been working on this matter, doing research and coming up with projects for a long time.

Since 2013 I have been guiding the design team at Paraşüt (www.parasut.com) which we founded together with Sean X. Yu and Andaç Türkmen. Paraşüt is a cloud- based application we developed with the vision of enabling small and medium scale enterprises, which have an important place in the economy in Turkey, to manage their financial operations more efficiently. The story of Paraşüt started with Sean's idea of creating an accessible application for small scaled enterprises. His idea is based on his past experience in finance sector and personal experiences as well. Sean persuaded Andaç for the software aspect and he made me believe in the idea with respect to the design part of the project. Upon this process, we started to work on the application. We set up Paraşüt by getting the investment aid from Revo Capital and developed the first version in which only purchase and sale invoices could be entered, the voices could be printed out and collections as well as payments could be tracked. Since that day, Paraşüt has been growing and developing with the investment support from Turkey and the Silicon Valley. For the time being, Paraşüt currently employs a total of 30 people who work in product development, design, marketing, sales and support teams. The application has now reached a maturation that can fulfill almost all the bookkeeping needs of small and medium sized enterprises (SMEs) which amount to 100.000. We also provide additional services such as electronic billing, online collection by credit card and transferring data automatically by bank integration; hence, we are trying to facilitate the financial operations of our customers by means of technology.

Turkey is in fact a country, which has a rooted history in terms of accounting software. There are comprehensive accounting programs developed dating back to a long time ago. The innovation Paraşüt has brought to this area is the accessibility aspect. Being a cloud-based application, Paraşüt does not necessitate a setup, there is no hardware cost involved, it is constantly updated, it is easy to understand and use so it does not require any training or accounting experience.

What is your opinion on the significance and the future of user experience from the perspective of illusional marketing?

I read an article which was about the fact that people were afraid of using the metro when the London Underground tube was constructed. The metro had an unpleasant atmosphere, it was dark, smelly and too hot in the summer. Despite being developed as an assertive solution to the unbearable traffic problem of the city, the metro did not prove to be as effective as it had been expected. This situation continued to be like this until the experience of "traveling under the ground" was designed completely from scratch. The sensation of getting under the ground was reduced by better ventilation and lighting systems. Besides, through a clean, hygienic and organized corporate image, the feeling that elicits the impression of everything being under control and reliable was created. A similar story can be told for the commercial airline companies that emerged 80 years after the London metro. The "traveling by plane" experience designed end-to-end in detail is as far as possible from the reality of the incident itself. You sip your coffee, read your newspaper and you cover kilometers of distance by flying as if it is quite "normal" to do so.

Today, unconventional business ideas like Airbnb and Uber offer a satisfactory experience by being designed end-to-end. Through this kind of experience, these ideas have been adopted by large masses and become a part of our daily lives. When I consider the user experience design within this context, I think that this matter will play a vital role in the advent of technologies such as *virtual reality* and *artificial intelligence* into our daily lives in the future.

What does "Design that doesn't make you think" mean for Paraşüt?

The computer literacy and competence that enterprise owners who have mingled with technology have acquired in their daily lives are very important for us. It is these people who are in the primary target audience of Paraşüt.

A cloud-based application in our day consists of the integration of many various micro interactions including logging in, logging out, searching, filtering, viewing details, filling out forms, creation of records, editing, deleting and all that. We try hard to use these micro interactions in their most conventional and habitual forms so as to help with the easy completion of complicated accounting operations within Paraşüt. Even though the users are unfamiliar with the application, they can make out what will happen when they click on a certain feature as a result of their previously acquired knowledge. Of course, it is necessary that you understand what the application is capable of doing to be able to use the application to a particular end. Paraşüt is an application which provides assistance to its users with many bookkeeping tasks. Therefore, understanding what the user wants to do and enabling the user to start doing that is of critical importance to grasp the value of the application. By making the basic tasks come to the fore in a main menu and providing the users who visit the application for the first time with guidance that is spared from the technical terms as much as possible, we assist them so that they can start the task they want to do. After the user starts the task she wants to do, it is required that she follow a few minor operations within a certain flow and order so that the outcome can be achieved. Following each operation, it is important that the next operation is visible. Therefore, we pay attention to the fact that there is only one single button that comes to the fore on the screen. In cases where we deem necessary, we provide the users with relevant information through the help contents so that they can proceed. Only when you can make the user do a task through the required directions and assistance, it means that you have been able to achieve a difficult objective and teach something new to that user. If you keep the same design fiction in other tasks that could be performed within the application, the user becomes capable of doing those tasks. Therefore, the more consistent your design fiction is within the application, the easier it will be to learn it. For instance, you have to click "customers" on the main menu to add a new customer to Paraşüt. Then, you need to click the "Add New Customer" button that merely comes to the forefront on the screen. Then, you will have to fill out the form and click the "Save" button which also comes to the forefront as the only feature. The same fiction applies for the operation of other items such as sale invoices, cost receipts and invoices, employees and bank accounts. It is possible to access them all from the same main menu and you can find the "add new" and "save" buttons in the same places indicated in the same color. If the user is satisfied with the task the application has performed and returns to do the same task once again, then this user becomes our customer and long-lasting relationship is also initiated in this way. The customers of Paraşüt use the application four days a week on average and in this way, they get to know the character of Paraşüt. We have some customers who identify Paraşüt as an assistant. The reason for this is that as the team who developed Paraşüt, we always try hard not to contradict with the decisions we have made earlier and we develop all the new features added into the application in a way that is congruent and consistent with the design, architecture, configuration and vision of Paraşüt. Thus, our customers can view Paraşüt as an assistant they are familiar with, they trust and whose reactions they may figure out.

How do you think the ideal user experience should be?
What information can you share with us you do as Paraşüt regarding the ideal user experience?

We have observed that the importance of synchronization and co-operation between the teams during the rapid growth of Paraşüt increased in direct proportion with the size of the company. I believe that the user experience is a holistic issue and the aggregate (total) of all the interactions of a user with Paraşüt constitutes the user experience. From this perspective, a potential customer of Paraşüt can see the advertisements that the marketing team has devised, get information from the website which the brand communication and design team are working on, use the application, get in touch with someone involved in the customer service team or speak with one of our customer representatives. As can be seen, all the departments have responsibility with regard to presenting an ideal experience to the customers. All of the departments are involved in communication with the customers and they try to offer the best service they can to the customers. At this point, it is also of crucial value that all departments share their education, training outcomes and experiences they have acquired with the other departments at Paraşüt. For example, it is important that the support team gets informed in due time about the features that have recently been developed. Likewise, the product development team learns about the parts of the product which cause the most difficulty while using it from the support team. Furthermore, the marketing team provides information regarding the expectations of the users who have started to put the product into practice, while the sales team conveys the customer demands to the product team. All similar interdepartmental flow enables us to improve Paraşüt and the experience we offer to our customers on a regular basis.

References

36. Norman, Don, & Nielsen, Jacob. "The Definition of User Experience." Nielsen Norman Group. Accessed 23 Sept 2016. https://www.nngroup.com/articles/definition-user-experience/

37. Maeda, John. *The Laws of Simplicity*. Cambridge: MIT Press, 2006.

38. Norman, Donald, A. *The Design of Everyday Things: Revised And Expanded Edition*. New York: Basic Books, 2013.

39. Krug, Steve. *Don't Make Me Think!: A Common Sense Approach to Web Usability*. Pearson Education, 2000.

40. Seth, Jagdish N., Newman, Bruce I., & Gross, Barbara L. *Consumption Values and Market Choices: Theory and Application*. Cincinnati: South-Western, 1991.

41. Kotler, Philip. "Marketing Management: The millennium edition," *Marketing Management* 23:6 (2000), pp. 188-193.

42. Fry, Richard. "Millennials are the largest generation in the U.S. labor force." Accessed 15 May 2018. http://www.pewresearch.org/fact-tank/2015/05/11/millennials-surpass-gen-xers-as-the-largest-generation-in-u-s-labor-force/

PART 6

GAMIFICATION

> *"The real game is starting now as the smart devices, which measure the behaviors in the world of Internet of Things, also become 'players' themselves..."*
>
> *-- Michael Wu*

Attention Economy and Gamification

We have said engaging consumers is the most challenging problem for marketers in modern times. Amidst the communication bombardment of the information age, it would be a naïve attitude to expect customers to bother interacting with your brand by means of old marketing methods. In fact, it is important to boost the motivation of the consumers so that you can get them to interact. Realizing gamification by adding the game mechanics into the existing processes to increase motivation is a method whose efficiency has been verified. And it is the digitalization itself which renders it possible to add gamification into the game plots in real life. Unless you digitize something and measure it, you cannot develop it, nor will you be able to construct the game plot over it.

Days that are even more interesting than today are awaiting us with regard to the information explosion. Machine to machine communication, named M2M, and the Internet of Things convey a vision smart machines share with people through their processing of data obtained by very different sensors. It is predicted that the number of sessions opened by machines on the internet will be 60 times more than the sessions opened by human users by 2020, which is not that far at all.

From smart automobiles to smart cities, smart homes to smart watches, the Internet of Things has been penetrating into all areas of our lives, and through this way, the game arena will be much broader. When everything is measured, *much richer (more based on information), more meaningful (healthy living, healthy sleeping, healthy eating, etc.) and more holistic* gamification plots will be put into practice.

In an era when the amount of knowledge is increasing at a rapid pace and has reached a level which is not easy to deal with, gamification could be an imperative. Amidst such abundance of information, which information people should focus on in that particular time frame and the level they are supposed to carry a particular thing would mean nothing but information pollution without structures like dashboards in games that display the information and the indicators that are required.

Now, let's analyze concepts of game and gamification in detail.

The Concept of Game

Games are as old as the existence of human beings. Games and learning through games is a method that has been resorted to for a long time particularly for subject matters that require learning by experiencing. While playing a game, the players feel that they are in a different environment than they actually are in real life. In addition, during the games, people would feel more comfortable to display behaviors they would in fact avoid manifesting in real life situations, thus, they can get the results of their behaviors or manage the learning process by making different decisions compared to those they would make in real life instances.

Entertaining and teaching game environments have been on the increase both for children and also for adults. 18 % of the world population and 25 % of the population in Turkey play a digital game per day.[43]

When the details of gamers in Turkey are analyzed in percentage, it is observed that 60 % of the population pays for the game they play. As

---

[43] Yusuf Yavuz, Türkiye'nin yüzde 25'i dijital oyun oynuyor, 2014 (accessed 23 Sept 2016). http://www.dha.com.tr/turkiyenin-yuzde-25i-dijital-oyun-oynuyor_735664.html

it is the case in most sectors, we are in the position of being consumers, not producers in the gaming sector as well. [44]

Games are defined as: "a form of entertaining activity that improves skill and intelligence, which has certain rules and helps one to have a good time. Accordingly, games are structured systems that make players race within the framework of certain rules that exist with the outcome of winning or losing, entailing motivation in its infrastructure and have players take action through the relevant feedback.

What does a Game Involve?

- **System:** Game is a platform on which the boundaries of the game environment and what can be done within this environment are known by the users themselves.
- **Players:** Player is the person who is to interact both with the elements of the game and with the other players in the game environment in compliance with the relevant rules.
- **Competition:** This entails the targets assigned to the players involved in the game environment.
- **Rules:** Based on the game elements being used while playing the game, rules must be equal and open for everyone. In this way, the game can be fair and its results will be acceptable.
- **Interaction:** Interaction is the communication players are engaged in with other players who are in the game in exchange of the missions they undertake. Communication can serve the purposes of competition or support.
- **Feedback:** Players receive informative, motivating interaction with regard to the moves they make or they receive some warning signals about the mistakes they make, all of which fall into the category of feedback.

---

[44] Oyunder, "Turkish gaming market" (accessed 23 Sept 2016).
http://www.slideshare.net/OYUNDER/turkish-gamingmarketinfografi-kapril3pay

- **Outcomes:** Outcomes are the structures which enable the players to see the levels and parts they have proceeded, the skills acquired and the people they have been able to defeat.
- **Emotional motivation:** This is the sine qua non of the game. Although all the plots have been aptly integrated, the game cannot proceed if the player does not show the required motivation or willingness to play. In the background, what we are to aim at should always be the emotions.

The Common Features of Games

There are shared features in all games including football, basketball, chess and car races. These common features are:

- A common ultimate target
- Open rules
- Instant feedback
- Voluntary participation

These four common features in the games come to the fore as the most basic ones regarding games and gamification in the physical and virtual world.

For instance, LinkedIn asks for its users to enter information such as their résumé, educational background, professional experience and similar details concerning themselves onto the platform. This target is the ultimate goal of the LinkedIn company. To the extent the user enters his / her input, LinkedIn can show the extent the user has completed his / her profile by means of the progress bar. This indication is realized as an instant feedback. Along with the progress bar, what percentage of profile completion will be achieved if you enter a particular piece of information is shared as the open rules with the user (for example, profile completion will go up by 10 % if you enter your educational background).

Gamification

Game, as a closed process in itself, is a practice governed by rules, which have targets like winning and losing, and aim at making people have fun, socialize and learn as well.

Gamification, on the other hand, is a multidisciplinary approach that can be defined as a mechanism design in which game mechanics are added into a process external to the game, which in itself is not a practice, and turns the participants into players within this process and enables their participation via motivation. If we are to compare games and gamification in a nutshell, the table provided below can shed light on such a comparison:

Table 5: Comparison of the Concepts of Game and Gamification

Game	Gamification
It involves objects and rules concerning their use.	Rules mostly serve for the fulfillment of tasks.
It involves winning and losing.	Losing is not generally the case. It is supported more to get someone to take action.
It has a story and a design in line with the story.	It supports whatever process it is practiced for.
It should be designed entirely and should work on its own.	It is integrated into the existing process and its mechanics work separately.
Its production is very expensive and complicated.	Its integration is easy.

Good Examples: Gamification in Real Life

In all realms of our lives in which there are scores, points, different statuses and badges, leadership boards, a pleasant competition and rewards, we may say that the processes have been gamified.

Gamification in Education

University entrance exams are an example of gamification accompanied by competition in academic life both for students themselves and universities whose base scores have been established. Grading system in the curriculum of an educational institution entails a system that has been gamified by being weighed against certain dimensions of the teacher of the course that guides the students to study (i.e. through attendance, projects, midterm and final exam) and gives a *score*.

Similarly, each university gamifies the process of employing faculty members like assistant professors, associate professors and professors in line with certain eligibility criteria for academics such as having delivered presentations for the proceedings at international conferences, having written a certain number of papers for certain indexed journals by scoring the points the university attaches importance to.

You can also apply the rewards in a plot that you have gamified yourself. For example, when I complete the weekly tasks on my planner before the deadline, I reward myself through some small treats like having a rest for a couple of hours by getting away from daily chores. This really works for me to complete the tasks promptly.

✓ The Fierce Competition on Social Media

Imagine the profiles on social networking sites such as Facebook and Instagram. You can feel the game and competition in all of their aspects. When we see a friend of ours who has uploaded a very attractive profile photo, we start to have this inner dialogue: "What do I lack that he / she has? I must get a much better photo taken and upload it." The status, the schools we graduated from, the company we are working for, how many followers we have and how many people have liked our posts' become the reasons for boasting and self-praise. A mass has already formed, made up of people who have entrapped themselves within an artificial virtual world for the mere purpose of increasing the number of their followers and keeping up pretty appearances for those followers. Some of them manage to confess what they have done after getting bored with this artificial game that does not make any sense at all. It is also possible to observe that some of them even commit suicide due to the fastidiousness, meaninglessness and pointlessness of the life they have so far led.

✓   Examples of Classical Gamification

An example of gamification that has been applied for many years is the boarding passes of airline companies that save miles. The system which helps the user to buy a new ticket as a result of the flight miles accumulated is quite motivating for those who travel frequently. Yet, in ideal gamification, it is important not to target only one specific audience or customer mass but offer a motivating carrot for the other types of "players" as well.

In similar fashion, some coffee chains stamp on the blank slots of the cards given to their customers for each coffee the customer buys. These cards have 10 slots, and when the stamped slots amount to 10, the coffee chain gives one cup of coffee free of charge. In such a case, 'players' who hardly ever drink coffee will not be motivated at all to use the system. An experiment conducted in this subject matter is quite interesting. A coffee brand has tried a second variation of the system which offers a coffee reward as a result of the same number of purchases. As an alternative to the card with 10 slots as it was the case in the earlier practice, they decided to hand out a card with 12 slots, three of which will be stamped on. Although the same number of purchases would be required to get a free cup of coffee, seeing that the first three slots are stamped and full on the 12-slot card at the initial stage has formed a kind of perception in the customer's brain that he has already made some progress along his way towards the target. Thus, it has been revealed that this procedure with the 12-slot card will make the customer be more motivated to realize the remaining required purchases. As can be figured out from this example, feedback mechanisms that make one feel that the process is making a progress such as the progress bars always work. Another similar and evident example is the progress bar we see when the operating system installed in our computer is turned on. When we see the progress bar, our patience coefficient increases.

Figure 6.1 A Typical Loyalty Card

✓ Objects also Take Part in Games

One of the reasons why such techniques, which have been employed for decades, have remained to be primitive is that it was not possible to access much information about customers during the years when these systems began to be used. Yet, today microchips have become more affordable and compact as well and they can be inserted into anything. Besides, sensor technology has seen significant advancements. All these factors have led to the internet of things where each object has become a *"smart player"* itself.

Micheal Wu, in the interview we had with him, states the following:

"In the world of the internet of things, objects such as smart wristbands, boilers and automobiles which measure all the behaviors in a digital medium are in fact players themselves. And the real game is only at its initial stage."

✓ Gamification in Insurance Business

The Association of British Insurers implemented a new gamified system in which vehicle owners can participate on a voluntary basis if they wish to be involved in the system. The owners of vehicles who are willing to use the system install a device in their cars. By means of the sensor, this device is able to track to what extent the drivers abide by the speed limits within a year, whether they corner in a risky manner or not as well as their habits concerning accelerating and braking suddenly. It also reports all these acts to the center. Enabling the driver to follow up his own performance via the web-based indicator console, this system allows some insurance premium discount at the end of the year based on the *score* assigned to the driver.

The Psychology of Game

During the period when the word gamification was not that well-known, experts who were working on this subject matter grounded in psychology and took into account the background of the business. Accordingly, they put forth definitions such as "*Implementing Behavior Change through Motivation*". Definitions that outline the essence of the subject matter fall into this framework. The word gamification was first coined by Gabe Zichermann. In the opening speech of the first gamification conference which was held back in 2010, Zichermann uttered these: "75 % of gamification is psychology and 25 % is technologies. " Therefore, the game mechanics that you use, its designs and your plots should absolutely have psychological references and allusions.

> *In marketing, rather than the old techniques that have lost their power and turned out to be ineffective, behavioral psychology has started to be employed more and more each day.*

Fogg Model

Professor B. J. Fogg, one of the faculty members of Stanford University, has proven himself to be the most prominent contemporary representatives of behavioral psychology of all time. Named "**The *Fogg Behavior Model***", his approach complements Skinner's approach, explaining what leads to change in behavior. Fogg's Model addresses three aspects. According to this model, motivation, ability and triggers should concurrently come together for a behavior change to occur.

If the gamification design does not work, these three elements need to be reevaluated, and one has to identify which element needs to be changed or improved. Gamification design should be readjusted in line with such an evaluation. In other words, if the gamer does not have the required motivation, it is expected that he / she will take action once he / she receives an instance of feedback. With the feedback received at the end of the action, it is anticipated that the player will be even more motivated. If the player is not motivated at all, then he / she will not take action. If he / she is motivated, there will be no action taken either unless there is the right feedback or reinforcer.

For the targeted behavior change, it is essential that motivation and action rise and along with these, there should be support through reinforcers. Hope, accepting / being accepted and getting pleasure are factors which elevate motivation, whereas elements such as non-routine loops, money, time and reward reinforce the ability component, namely the desire to do.

The Key to Turn Behavior into Habit: Tiny Habits

The theory of tiny habits developed by the game designer B. J. Fogg states that habits that are under the control of the unconscious have an extraordinarily powerful impact on our behaviors. According to this theory, in order to convert a new behavior into a habit, the best way to be followed would be to articulate some different behaviors, tiny habits, into the deepseated behaviors in our daily lives. According to Eyal, habits are behaviors, or small actions, which are done either with little or no conscious thought. They are formed by frequency or attitude change like altering the perception regarding the behavior. These habits are usually taken for granted. To illustrate, if you complain about the fact that you cannot allocate time to call your mother under the intense work pressure of your daily life and if you have already formed a habit of having a coffee every day at a certain time interval, you may condition yourself to phone your mother the moment you place your coffee mug on your desk. When you do this about twenty times, getting your coffee will turn into being a trigger signal for you to call your mother. Thus, this new behavior which you have articulated will start to emerge in the autopilot mode completely as a habit. This theory highlights the significance of the unconscious and autopilot behavior which the illusional marketing techniques rest on.

Behaviorism is evaluated under the circumstances of our day with the guidance of Dan Ariely, who has been conducting research particularly on the realm of economy. In his book, *Predictably Irrational*, he states that people display a basic behavior that can be predicted all the time; brain and intelligence guide our choices and behaviors by coming into play only after a long time or at some instances brain and intelligence do not ever come into play[45]. Behaviors we display like winking, moving our hand away from a hot source or changing our direction when we hear an explosion also guide us in instances that have to do with the economy.

A critically important psychological system lies underneath the background of gamification. And it is most of the time these instances and realms which merely rely on the "add point, give a badge" approach, which is deemed to turn ineffective in the long run.. The code that is capable of putting the people's behavioral routines into a loop within a system through the right reinforcers can be found in such theorems and components, and this has been pointed out by Pavlov, Skinner, Fogg as well as Dan Ariely.

Intrinsic Motivation - Extrinsic Motivation

Even though reward happens to be the most important psychological infrastructure component in gamification, what is powerful in fact is the game mechanics. And yet, there are occasionally instances in which reward may preclude motivation and behavior change. Let's assume that you are supposed to construct a "quit-smoking gamification" in the sense of social responsibility. Generally, what springs to mind is a display in the form of a *progress bar* which includes the disruption of series as one smokes throughout the days on which the smoker reduces the number of cigarettes or a score that is assigned for each day the person has not smoked a cigarette. It could also be a Green Crescent badge for those who can complete one month without smoking. "It goes quite well, but what

---

[45] Dan Ariely, *Predictably Irrational: The Hidden Forces That Shape Our Decisions,* HarperCollins, 2008.

about the reward?" Yet, a monetary reward or another materialistic one like a car would involve a person in the game even if he does not intend to quit smoking at all but indeed needs money and a car. In this case, the car will be an extrinsic motivator in its fullest sense. The points earned and badges would not attract the attention of many players; what they would focus on would be the reward itself, so they might even forget the fact that they have been competing for the sake of giving up smoking.

As the research reveals, if the reward gets ahead of the whole process and the other game mechanics within the process, this will be done only for extrinsic motivation and as it will not be internalized, no behavior change would be experienced, which means the person would not quit smoking after the reward is won or lost. The user who has not smoked during the competition for the sake of the reward would pay keen attention to this inner voice of his / hers: "That was for the car, now I can light a cigarette and enjoy it." This means the user will lose the real game and also the gamification. Here comes into play this issue which points to one of the most important losses concerning gamification.

Intrinsic motivation, on the other hand, refers to the fact that the player is really intent to do it but somehow he / she cannot realize it. These may include some examples like healthier eating, doing sports and saving money. It is possible to come up with successful gamification that would work, live and develop with the right game mechanics and plot geared towards a player who already has the intrinsic motivation. The differing aspects between intrinsic motivation and extrinsic motivation are mostly elucidated through making money. We all have to make a living and we work in a way for that particular purpose. In fact, waking up early, working overtime, nonsensical disagreements and required meetings are all realities surrounding business life. Even if we do not like all of these chores, we are supposed to put up with this situation for the sake of some gain like "salary" along with the related extra benefits. And yet, in our free time, while playing Monopoly, let's say, we wish to live in a better neighborhood by gaining more valuable assets and earning money in the game. Thus, we try to do whatever is required.

Gamification which is oriented towards extrinsic motivation might work in the short-term but as it is in the case of quitting smoking, this usually ends up with failure in the long-run. How can we turn this into intrinsic motivation? First of all, make sure that the reward is something that complements and supplements your process. The reward for giving up smoking should not be the car, rather it should be a complimentary reward like a vacation, a sports club membership or a scuba diving course that will support a healthy lifestyle.

The Target Audience in Gamification

One of the most elements of gamification is the players who play the game. Players are defined as participants who are willing to be a part of the game. It is important to initiate the process by being aware of the fact that not all players are the same in terms of taking part in the game, expectations and motivation. For these reasons, it is important that you analyze your target players very carefully and efficiently.

Target player profiles are critical in the gamification process. "Bartley's Player Types" developed by Bartley in 1996 have been acknowledged broadly in the literature[46]. In Bartley's taxonomy, there is a classification with four player types: Killers, Achievers, Socializers and Explorers.

Player Types

1. Killers: They make up a small portion of players, corresponding to 1%. They are focused on other players, instead of being engaged in the rules, progression and tasks of the game. They strive to beat the other players. They want to eliminate their rivals without paying attention to specific rules or how rules are to be applied. While beating off rivals, they do not care if their moves are in compliance with the rules or not.

2. Achievers: Players in this category can be considered "a man of duty". As long as such players achieve their mission, they do not see any problem in the achievements of other players. These players are result-oriented and they want to see their progress status while completing each level as

---

[46] Richard Bartle, "Hearts, clubs, diamonds, spades: Players who suit MUDs," *Journal of MUD Research* 1:1 (June 1996). https://mud.co.uk/richard/hcds.htm

quickly as possible. If the mission is at 90% and they have to quit playing the game, they fulfill the mission first and then quit the game.

3. Socializers: Just like the Killer category, this group is also interested in other players. Yet, their goal is not to beat the other players; they rather wish to gain in-game aspects together with the others. Moreover, they enjoy getting help from others by using mechanics like chat feature, making progress as a team and leadership boards, which are all to do with other players. Upon a very small progress, they are inclined to share this progress with the other players or make an acquaintance with a new player during the game instead of moving on with the game.

4. Explorers: Players in this category are interested in the game itself rather than the missions of the game or the other players. They enjoy exploring all the areas of the game. Hidden realms are particularly appealing to this category of game players.

Finding out which Player Category your Customers Fall into

It is essential that you probe into the player category your customers fall into so that the future gamification design can be a successful one. If there are more than one persona card at stake, then you have to conduct the same process separately for each customer type.

> *You can administer the survey found at the link below so that you can find out which category of player type your customers fall into:*
> *https://bit.ly/2olBV9H*

Marczewski[47] provides a little more detailed definition of player types. That model also provides what kind of a game is required to be constructed for each player type. Most of the player types are the same as what Bartley proposed as player types.

---

[47] Andrzej Marczewski, *Gamification: A Simple Introduction*, 2013.

- Player: Type of player, a typical player mass.
- Free spirit: Players in this category prefer to play the game in line with their own rules and have it their own way. It is possible to keep such players in the play by offering them some unexpected rewards, secret and hidden badges.
- Disruptors: These players can easily be distracted. In order to keep them in the play, it would be wise to set an environment in which comments are made constantly, minor instances of feedback are provided. Besides, with a kind of anarchy created in the game, the players would go on playing without keeping their eyes off the game.
- Philanthropist: Players who fall into this category contribute to the other players and game mechanics without expecting any benefit in return and they all do this voluntarily. Their biggest motivation is to make people happy and it would be an appropriate strategy to give this group of players plenty of rewards.

After you get to know your player well, the next step is to identify what kind of gamification mechanics would be appropriate to apply within the specific context in line with the selected target audience. Yet, what is going to be gamified also plays a determining role in the mechanics to be applied. In some instances, competitive gamification scenarios can be carried on, which renders an efficient process design possible. In some other cases, such a competitive scenario may have an adverse impact. For example, in a research we conducted in 2015, it was observed that competitive strategy did not work in the long run and had negative effects since many students withheld themselves and started to take a dislike to the education process. While this was the case with competitive strategies, it was observed that a cooperative gamification brought about more meaningful and efficient outcomes.[48]

---

[48] Adnan V. Ertemel & Volkan Sel, "The Role of Gamification in Online Learning Management Systems," 7th International Conference of Strategic Research on Social Science and Education (ICoSReSSE), 2017.

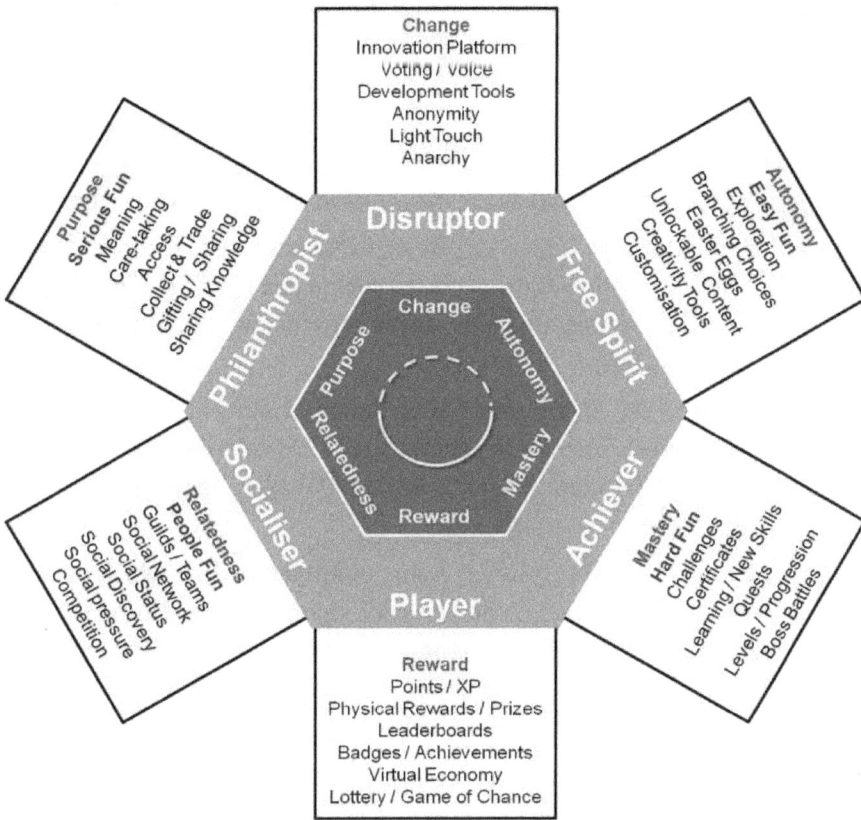

Figure 6.3: Marczewski's Player Types

Types of Entertainment in Gamification

After conducting the analysis into who the target audience is, what kind of players they are and what motivates them, it is important to examine the elements that entertain different types of players. "4 Keys 2 Fun" model developed by Lazzaro in this respect provides a categorization of entertainment types.[49] The basic dimensions taken as basis in this model used in the

---

[49] Nichole Lazzaro, Why we play games: Four keys to more emotion without story, 2014. https://twvideo01.ubm-us.net/o1/vault/gdc04/slides/why_we_play_games.pdf

types of entertainment that motivate Marczewski's player types are dscribed below:

1) Hard Fun: The plot of the game makes it hard to win. This type of entertainment makes the player have fun as progress happens.

2) Easy Fun: This is an easy form of entertainment the purpose of which is to allow the players to unwind and have fun. Role playing and simulations are some of the choices that could be resorted to in this form.

3) People Fun: This form of entertainment aims at making people accomplish something together with others and have fun while doing so. Teamwork and having multi players can be preferred in this form of entertainment.

4) Serious Fun: This involves a sort of entertainment which has the purpose of having some behavior change in players and making them learn something rather than merely having fun. Some ex- amples are used in the serious fun form and the goal is to have players learn certain things after they complete the game.

It is aimed that the people who are involved in the gamification process will each turn into " a participant" by taking part in some small games before becoming customers. Those who prefer instant piano stairs remain in the "participant" level in the Fun Theory (see the Piano stairs video). Processes which involve a longer time period, rules and interaction with other players will be the next level. Afterwards, such "participants" will have the motivation and be willing to have full knowledge of all the mechanics, innovative aspects and the entire plot of the game. They turn into individuals who play the game and get others to play the game, namely they become "players". And it is through such a transformation that you will have completed the "gamification" process to a great extent.

The SAPS Rewards Theory

When we generalize gamification design as sorting out the prob- lems that emerge along a process by providing motivation, then the most important reinforcer would be the *"reward"* that is capable of generating motivation in the users from the very beginning till the end. Giving rewards in the same way throughout the whole process is one of the biggest common mistakes. While materialistic rewards can be provided at the initial stages to generate extrinsic motivation, later on it will be necessary to provide rewards that are related to and supplementary for the process so that the players can realize internalization with regard to the relevant actions. Otherwise, the actions that are enacted for the reward will result in extinction once reward saturation occurs or the reward disappears.

The well-known gamification expert Gabe Zichermann (www.gamification.co) made an analysis of reward types in four dimensions, which is recognized on a wide-scale.

Status	• Levels
	• Badges
	• Ranks
Access	• Privillage
	• Reach
Power	• Moderator
	• Enforcer
	• Editor
Stuff	• Discounts
	• Giveaways
	• Deals

Figure 6.4: The SAPS Theory

Stuff: Stuff involves providing the user with materials that are tangible or can be converted into cash or traded for money as a reward; if not, it includes giving the users rewards that they can purchase with money or by other means.

Power: Power involves conferring some kinds of 'power', in other words some rights, to the users either during the game or to ones who have just started playing the game. The primary goal in doing so is to get the users to adopt the system. For example, if you are a mayor on Foursquare-Swarm, you have the right to do arrangements on the photos and reviews related to the particular venue.

Access: Access can be defined as information, venue or devices that are not open to the access or use of regular players but they can be accessed by the owners of the system or by people with higher status. VIP lounges at the airports can be given an example to describe access. In gamifications in the workplace, examples of access could be taking part in a meeting held by the executives of the company or being involved in a project that is not disclosed. A dinner with the CEO could be given as another example of access.

Status: The most appropriate level and the one that supports intrinsic motivation is the *status* level. It involves some parts of the system to be managed by the users by assigning some of the roles in the system to the users so that they can perform management and follow up with that title or status. In addition to this, they are rewarded in return. The verified accounts on Twitter, the badges given to the contents that have been fully completed on Linkedin, the right to be an author on Ekşisözlük and the *expert title* given to the good users in the system are some examples that illustrate the status.

The Linking of Gamification with Storytelling and User Experience: The Dynamics, Mechanics and Components of Games

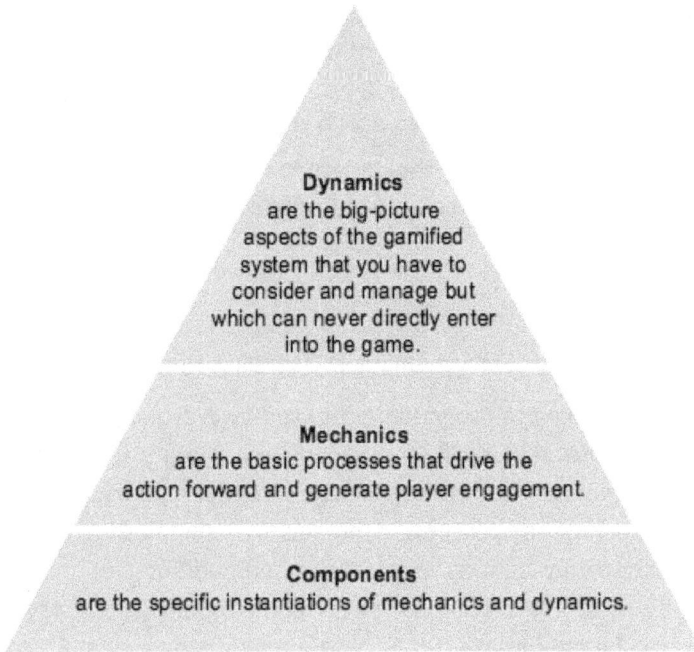

Dynamics
are the big-picture
aspects of the gamified
system that you have to
consider and manage but
which can never directly enter
into the game.

Mechanics
are the basic processes that drive the
action forward and generate player engagement.

Components
are the specific instantiations of mechanics and dynamics.

Instantiation-Design Related
Figure 6.5: The Gamification Toolkit: Dynamics, Mechanics, Components.
Source: Werbach & Hunter (2012)

Werbach and Hunter model argues that in gamification it is necessary to start with the structural dimension, which is to say constructing the dynamics of the game. Although the visible aspects in games are elements such as points, badges and leadership boards seem to be like the entire game, it is not possible to get a favorable result through a sort of gamification that lacks mechanics which provide the motivation in the background of the game and that is devoid of dynamics which the game basically rests on.

Game mechanics are design solutions that enable the players to internalize the subject matter and that are independent of the rules of the game that impact the whole gamification environment. Based on the dynamics of the game, mechanics of the game are elements that nurture the components that the end user sees. It is also the part which the user gets involved in an entire interaction with the application. To recap, while components refer to the part that is visible to the players, dynamics refer to the part that is felt and mechanics to the aspect that is experienced.

The Importance of Storytelling and User Experience in Gamification

According to the model proposed by Werbach and Hunter, it is the game dynamics that have strategic value in gamification design and that should be planned from the very beginning. Storytelling is stated to be the most important among these dynamics. The significance of storytelling in gamification can be seen in the theory named Self Determination developed by Ryan and Deci. This theory is a part of positive psychology and proves to be an important theory for gamification as well.[50] Autonomy, a meaningful purpose and mastery, according to this theory, make up the main components of intrinsic motivation. The foremost one among these elements is a lofty and meaningful aim, that is to say the story and its purpose.

Proceeding from the model of Werbach and Hunter, game components refer to the game elements that users see and interact with. This dimension is the projection of user experience in the games. Education scientist Jane McGonial notes that anyone aged 20-21 is an expert in the field of game in line with the 10000 hours rule of Gladwell. Visual elements in the games carry universal meanings. For instance, everyone knows what x sign in red or tick symbol in green color means. In such widely-recognized rules in user experience, language of gamification is employed quite extensively. Correspondingly, components are named directly as aesthetics in

---

[50] Richard M. Ryan & Edward L. Deci, "Self-determination theory and the facilitation of intrinsic motivation, social development, and well-being," *American Psychologist*, 55:1 (2000), p 68.

different gamification models (Zichermann,[51] Hunicke,[52] Kapp[53]). This nomination is in a way an indicator that demonstrates how this dimension is nested with the user experience design.

The Key to Success in Gamification: Sustainable and Meaningful Design

Games make things enjoyable when a target that requires patience to accomplish is at stake.

Progress bars, points, determination to go on with the routine without disrupting the series are some of the motivators that enable players to manifest perseverance. On the other hand, gamification whose plot has been constructed in a mindless way might yield an outcome in the short term; yet, humankind that has acquired immunity to everything in time by being adjusted to new circumstances will eventually sense such practices and put a mental block into action very quickly. Just like the case of email marketing at the beginning which caused spam email owing to people with ill-intentions, in time, ethical guidelines were developed, and this will inevitably be the case for gamification that will also be governed by ethical guidelines regarding the way and the dosage of implementing it.

Meaningful and Sustainable Gamification: NikeFuel

[51] Gabe Zichermann & Christopher Cunningham, *Gamification by Design: Implementing Game Mechanics in Web and Mobile Apps,* O'Reilly Media Inc., 2011.

[52] Robin Hunicke, Marc LeBlanc & Robert Zubek, "MDA: A formal approach to game design and game research," in *Proceedings of the AAAI Workshop on Challenges in Game AI,* Vol. 4, No. 1, 2004.

[53] Karl M. Kapp, *The Gamification of Learning and Instruction: Game-Based Methods and Strategies for Training and Education,* John Wiley & Sons, 2012.

Together, Nike+ ran 431,649,376 mi

17363
Laps around the world

17205
Trash-talking challenges

16775152
Pounds burned

8560
Stronger Powersongs

What's happening now in Nike+

Figure 6.7: Sustainable Gamification: NikeFuelBand Example

GOOD EXAMPLES: THE DIGITAL REVOLUTION AND GAME

✓ **NIKE+ FUELBAND - THE INSIDE STORY**

The example of NikeFuel also shows the importance of making the goal meaningful for sustainability in gamification. Leading a more active and fitter life is one of the greatest desires of people today. It is possible to compare this target with the gamification Foursquare applied at the initial stages. In the game, if the carrot does not serve a more sublime and inspirational purpose related to the player's basic desires, then the players will get bored after a certain point and quit the game eventually.
https://youtu.be/1r5YoWLexEc

✓ **Volkswagen's Social Responsibility Project: The Fun Theory Applications**

164

The German automobile manufacturer Volkswagen uses applications that apply gamification in the marketing aspect of their business. These applications are also available on the website www.thefuntheory.com. The website features instant and short-term application examples of game elements in daily life without using any digital infrastructure.

✔ Speed Camera Lottery

A camera was installed at an intersection where accidents frequently took place in the US. Instead of penalizing drivers who exceeded the 30-mile speed limit, those who drive below the speed limit are allowed to participate in a lottery; and this is displayed on a billboard by sharing the instant speed of the drivers. This speed camera lottery application was chosen to be "the best adapting gamification application" of the year 2011.

✔ Apple Watch

Apple offers an enriched experience for smart watches, combined with applications produced by third parties. In this respect, the product proves to be the only 'smart watch' that can be used no matter how expensive it may be. The Medical ID – Medical Identity - is the section in which you enter data on your blood type, your allergies and whom to reach in case of an emergency. This section will also be available for first aid purposes on the phone lockscreen in case of an accident. I hope it will help save many lives and become a standard feature on every phone.

✔ SuperBetter

Jane McGonigal is a prominent name with a far-reaching and powerful approach to gamification. She plans to make people do the good work they wish to accomplish in their lives, not just through gamification elements, but further make them feel as if they are in a complete gaming environment and playing the game. In short, "Turn your life into a game," she says. In SuperBetter, you can follow some action maps that are already set or you have set for yourself, and proceed with actions under four main headings, i.e. physical, logical, emotional and social. Thus, you can make progress in accordance with the matter that is targeted.

✓ LinkedIn

LinkedIn is a social network for business professionals. By sharing their CVs online, users can add information concerning their education, previous work experiences, certificates and even hobbies. What's more, they can get in contact with relevant individuals, institutions as well as organizations. With these features, it creates added value through the analyses it can potentially conduct on big data by evaluating the information based on aspects like work, projects, educational status and hobbies that belong to its members. Of course, they do not neglect to offer a gamified profile to the users.

✓ Some Examples of AR & VR Based Games

Many devices that come into our lives thanks to the developments in technology open up brand new digital channels to us. *Wearable Technologies, the Internet of Things, Drones, 3D Printers* and many more...

All of these new emerging technologies open the door to brand new tracks for gamification. Let us explain these new areas with some examples which have already taken place today as well as those that are yet to come from a futuristic perspective. We shall also examine how they can be integrated into our gamification plots.

Augmented Reality, abbreviated as AR, is a kind of technology that excites us all and is now within our reach. For example, through a mobile application called "**Blippar**", which you can use on your smartphone and tablet, brands can move their products from the real world to a virtual one. It aims to augment the impact of reality by combining reality and virtuality.

The gaming industry also follows wearable technologies very closely. Being able to change the entire gaming experience, "Oculus Rift", in particular, provides its users with impressive new generation experiences enhanced with **Virtual Reality** technologies. The feeling of being immersed in the environment is generated through the effect designed by the device. Players perceive themselves as if they are in the game and field so they become an actual part of the whole plot. Such environments can provide great experiences of gaming, especially when supported with walking platforms and balance objects.

In early 2014, Facebook saw this potential power of **Oculus Rift** and bought the company for about $ 2 billion. This was Facebook's first investment in wearable technologies. In the acquisition statement, it shared examples of applications that could be created in sectors such as health, education and entertainment, like getting a spot in the front row at events such as concerts and football matches with the help of this technology. Making all these experiences that involve **virtual reality** technology compete, be promoted and shared, that is, gamifying them, in general, are among the opportunities that are yet to come.

When it comes to wearable technology, most people think of "**Google Glass**". Launched by Google as Project Glass, this revolutionary device has paved the way for a myriad of innovations. By using the glass of your glasses as a screen, you can access information on your surroundings and make a search on the Internet. You can take photos and shoot videos and share them instantly. You can also access the information you need. All very sensational...You can gamify everything you see. All sorts of things from cooking, to meet people and to movies you watch, have become a part of gamification.

In the TV series "**Black Mirror**", which takes place in the gamified future, a working system is set up for human beings so that they can generate energy by running since all the energy resources in the world have been exhausted. Points and avatars are added to increase production, that is, to make people run more. In this way, all your winnings are achieved via the avatar you are associated with and you earn points instead of money. A television program you watch, some food you eat, and even the elevator you use result in a certain level of drop in your points.

✓ Pokémon

Dressed in Pokémon design of the Niantic company's game named "Ingress", the game Pokémon Go poses a great potential for brands. It is an augmented reality game that has been developed over a period of 3 years and more than 12 million people play it on a daily basis. Of the gamification mechanics, *Avatar, storytelling, ownership, scarcity and inadequacy, cooperation, competition and challenge* have been used in a very effective way.

An Interview with Michael Wu, Data Scientist at Lithium Technologies, on Gamification

Thank you for taking the time to talk to us and for your contribution to the book. Would you like to tell us about yourself?

I hold a degree in Physics from Berkeley University. As the Chief Scientist at Lithium Technologies, I work on issues like how to analyze and use the information within the company. Some people call me "Data Scientist" but I think every scientist has specialized in the subject matter of data. I focus more on "Application Data". That is, I work with the output obtained here so as to guide human behaviors, which makes me get involved in the subject of *gamification*. We have various innovative products at Lithium Technologies. These products can be forum-style platforms where company employees can connect and feel free to *interact* with each other in a motivated manner. Regarding sales and marketing related to the company's products, we also work on planning behavioral changes by analyzing customer focus and behaviors.

As a hobby, I must say that I have developed an interest in photography too. I've been traveling around the world with my wife because of conferences and during those visits, I try to take some nice photos.

With the concept of Illusional Marketing, an approach is proposed in which storytelling, user experience and gamification are used to convince consumers who have become unresponsive in our age by addressing their unconscious. From this perspective, what is your opinion on storytelling, user experience design and gamification?

Indeed, it is becoming more and more difficult for brands to attract the consumers' attention in the face of increasingly competitive conditions and information flowing in from everywhere. At this point, it proves to be highly effective to present the brand to consumers as a part of a bigger cause. In this sense, brands should design the kind of stories in which consumers will not only express themselves but also discover themselves by using the brand.

From the same perspective, user experience design is perhaps a more vital concept than storytelling. 'Simplicity' is the main goal to be achieved at the heart of user experience. The problem here is that the concept of simplicity is quite a relative notion. Something that's simple for one does not necessarily have to be simple for someone else. We can describe simplicity this way: using as few resources as possible while performing a task. When it comes to what these resources are, we can classify them as cognitive, physical, scarce resources and adaptation resources. *Cognitive resources* refer to the mental effort that needs to be put in so as to fulfill a certain task. *Physical resources* may be diverse. *Scarce resources* are resources such as money, time and attention. Specialization in a subject (a person has to make a choice as it is practically impossible for that person to specialize in every single subject) and the number of permissions that can be taken from the user to take action on a subject can be included in this category. Last but not least, adaptability refers to the existence of norms and generally accepted rules in a subject matter, and to the fact that user experience is compatible and consistent with these norms and customary user routines.

When the gamification dimension is examined, we see that those who work in the field of gamification come from a few disciplines in the background. They are grouped into three main categories: game designers, behavioral scientists and individuals from business life. There is one fundamental issue that they all seem to miss out on, that is the *data dimension*. This is the dimension I am interested in. By analyzing the data, it is possible to measure the user behavior up to the finest detail on digital medium. Moreover, just like in the film *Minority Report*, it is also possible to predict even future behaviors based on this data. The question of utmost importance here is: is it possible to channel human behavior towards a desired direction? This is where gamification comes into play. Gamification is, in essence, feedback rather than motivation. Feedback may also have a demotivating effect. For example; although, on the one hand a product like Fitbit may demotivate someone who hasn't done enough walking that day compared to the average amount of calories burned by other people, on the other, it does actually encourage the desirable behavioral change. Gamification helps individuals focus on goals that they can attain through perseverance and in the long run. It allows consumers to fully perceive the long-term value of every single step they take without missing the big picture.

As for the concepts explained in Illusional Marketing, it is argued that it encourages people not to think and also makes them dumb. What are your views on that?

I disagree with the argument that these developments render us stupid. They actually help us get rid of unnecessary routine work and chores, save time and focus more on the jobs that can touch human beings. For example, when the calculator was invented, some people must have said that they could do four operations with a pencil and paper and that they would not need a calculator at all. However, the calculator does not make us stupid; on the contrary, it assists us with complicated operations. In coping with the more complex world of the future, new techniques and technologies will definitely be required to help us think less.

What do you think of the criticisms that gamification has been overused and that it has begun to cause a wave of reaction?

The use of gamification in a mindless way, unfortunately, brings with it the danger of gaming fatigue and resistance to gamification. Gamification should not be used arbitrarily unless it adds a real benefit and surplus value to the users, not to the brand.

So, what do you think are the most important trends in consumer behaviors?

Humankind has always had a *social* character since its existence. He uses sociability in his interactions. He shares what he has done with those around him, and asks for their opinions and suggestions. This has never changed and will not change. Thanks to new digital tools, social interaction has been rendered easier by eliminating distances.

On this digitalization adventure, what do you think awaits us in the future?

First of all, as I have mentioned above, sociality and therefore social media will continue to be the most fundamental and powerful tool of interpersonal interaction.

On the other hand, the fact that everything is measurable in the Internet of Things will bring hyper-relevance to the developed products. Recording all the movements of customers from every angle on an individual level with big data will ultimately enable the projection of each customer's uniqueness to the database. In segmentation, which is an essential concept of marketing, in contrast to the approach of putting customers in the same basket by grouping them, data with different dimensions will be examined and interpreted to differentiate each customer. It is relatively an easy task to identify the difference of everyone on an individual basis through data. The real dexterity and skill is to use this data to provide an authentic experience that other brands cannot. Accomplishing this task in the digital world is much easier than doing it in the physical one. In that respect, the philosophy of customer development is highly crucial. If your favorite color is blue, it is easy to paint the background blue on the websites you enter. However, if we try to adapt this to the physical world, it is not so possible to paint the walls with the same color in a store for each user every time it is visited. Just at this point, *augmented reality (AR)* and *mixed reality* technologies, which enable the fusion of the digital and physical worlds, will come into play. For the preferred color, a layer of those preferred colors will be displayed in the observed physical world. In this way, a completely personal experience will also be made possible in the physical world.

The Irresistible Power of Habits and Illusional Marketing

The human brain is a magnificent structure ...

As Charles Duhigg puts it in his book, *The Power of Habits*, the human brain constantly tends to turn routines into habits and thus render them automatic.[54] The purpose of this is to relax the mind by getting rid of these things and to spend its precious time on more meaningful undertakings that have a higher added value.

Maslow's hierarchy of needs also explains this process quite well. Individuals whose basic needs such as shelter, food and water are met pursue more meaningful needs that are higher within the pyramid over time.

---

[54] Charles Duhigg, *The Power of Habit: Why We Do What We Do in Life and Business*, Random House, 2012.

At the top, needs such as self-actualization, sustainable living and spiritual satisfaction come to the fore.

The philosophy of Marketing 3.0 also targets the top layer of the pyramid. At this point, the concept and the importance of a brand that consistently presents the promise of a consistent benefit in making the routines a habit come to the fore.

Going back to the power of habits, it is necessary to address the right brain, which represents the subconscious mind, and to speak the language of the right brain, that is, the discourse of intuition, motivation and passion, visual signs (elements in the games) and stories so that it can gain control and make the routine automatic.

Research on apes and rats has shown how routines become habitual. In the model to explain the habits, triggering is done through a signal or cue in order to activate the routine that is desired to be made automatic in the model. Once the routine has been established, a reward is integrated in order to encourage the brain to repeat this programmed task. The critical point, which allows the routine to become a loop and become a habit, is a distinctive and authentic cue which is hidden in the reward.

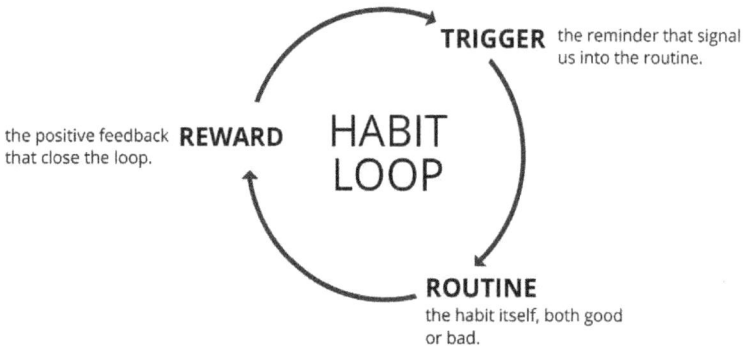

TRIGGER the reminder that signal us into the routine.

the positive feedback **REWARD** that close the loop.

HABIT LOOP

ROUTINE the habit itself, both good or bad.

Figure 6-8: The Habit Loop

The words cue and reward do not sound unfamiliar to you, do they? Yes, in games and gamified fiction, the ultimate aim is to encourage one to take a desired action with the evident cues and place a reward at the end of a routine in order to make it a habit that the subconscious programs. The fundamental psychology of gamification rests on this principle.

References

43. Yavuz, Yusuf. Türkiye'nin yüzde 25'i dijital oyun oynuyor. 2014. Accessed 23 Sept 2016. http://www.dha.com.tr/turkiyenin-yuzde-25i-dijital-oyun-oynuyor_735664.html

44. Oyunder. Turkish gaming market. Accessed 23 Sept 2016. http://www.slideshare.net/OYUNDER/turkish-gamingmarketinfografi-kapril3pay

45. Ariely, Dan. *Predictably Irrational: The Hidden Forces That Shape Our Decisions.* New York: HarperCollins, 2008.

46. Bartle, Richard. "Hearts, clubs, diamonds, spades: Players who suit MUDs," *Journal of MUD Research* 1:1 (June 1996).

47. Marczewski, Andrzej. *Gamification: A Simple Introduction,* 2013.

48. Ertemel, Adnan V., & Sel, Volkan. "The Role of Gamification in Online Learning Management Systems," 7th International Conference of Strategic Research on Social Science and Education (ICoSReSSE), 2017.

49. Lazzaro, Nichole. Why we play games: Four keys to more emotion without story, 2014. https://twvideo01.ubm-us.net/o1/vault/gdc04/slides/why_we_play_games.pdf

50. Ryan, Richard M., & Deci, Edward L. "Self-determination theory and the facilitation of intrinsic motivation, social development, and well-being," *American Psychologist*, *55*(1), 68, 2000.

51. Zichermann, Gabe & Cunningham, Christopher. *Gamification by Design: Implementing Game Mechanics in Web and Mobile Apps.* O'Reilly Media, Inc., 2011.

52. Hunicke, Robin, LeBlanc, Marc, & Zubek, Robert. MDA: A formal approach to game design and game research. In *Proceedings of the AAAI Workshop on Challenges in Game AI* (Vol. 4, No. 1). 2004.

53. Kapp, Karl M. *The Gamification of Learning and Instruction: Game-Based Methods and Strategies for Training and Education.* John Wiley & Sons, 2012.

54. Duhigg, Charles. *The Power of Habit: Why We Do What We Do in Life and Business.* Random House, 2012.

PART 7

THE OTHER SIDE OF THE COIN: THE ETHICAL DIMENSION OF ILLUSIONAL MARKETING

When we examine the current practices of marketing, we observe the fact that sometimes marketing managers are so self-centric that they have the sense of entitlement to waste the attention and time of the customers loutishly. Companies, which adopt such strategies, may seem to make profits in the short-term but they may jeopardize the trust of their customers in the long run...

The notions of trust and attention are scarce sources in terms of their nature. What's more, in this century, which is characterized by attention economy, these aforementioned notions have increasingly become more scarce and more significant as well. Having observed that the consumers do not or cannot pay attention to everywhere, the marketing world has started to resort to marketing techniques which take the unconscious as the basis. Yet, some practitioners in the field of marketing have started using these techniques inappropriately and untimely. Such illusional marketing techniques enable the development of habits through some behavioral patterns in the autopilot mode by making use of techniques whose efficiency has been proven since the beginning of the history of humanity.

The problem begins to emerge when the habits turn into addiction over time. These techniques in question are so effective in making people become glued to the screen that the companies in Silicon Valley have started to abuse this situation. Companies which implement the subtle tactics of behavioral psychology are in a keen competition to display the most successful examples of convincing design so that they can keep the consumers on the screen as long as and as much as possible at whatever cost it may take[55]. Having developed the Snapstreak feature by using gamification techniques, Snapchat provides a badge to the kids who text each other unceasingly for the number of days the kids texted one another. That is not the only thing Snapchat does. It also enables the users who are about to lose the badge to send messages by reminding them of how many remaining hours they have through an hourglass, which causes the users to panic and urges them to text so that their Snapstreak does not expire.

Figure 7.1: An Example of a Negative Gamification: Snapchat SnapStreaks

Young children who go on vacation with their families give their close friends their password so that those friends will send empty messages to the friends whom they text frequently for the sake of not losing the badge earned (?!). These rewards are so shallow but they prove to be sufficient to stimulate the part of the reward zone of the brain, amygdala, to secrete the dopamine hormone. This part of the human brain is prone to illusion as well. And this illusion not only works in the case of children but also of adults. The technique employed by Snapchat is known as the 'Hook' technique that is used to form experiences that promote habits.

---

[55] A. V. Ertemel & G. Aydın, "Technology Addiction in the Digital Economy and Suggested Solutions," *Addicta: The Turkish Journal on Addictions*, 5 (2018), 665-690.

175

Eyal, the author of the book *Hooked*, developed the hook model by adding the step of investment in the platform as the fourth step of the habit loop explained in the previous part of this book. Eyal recommends that marketing managers do not need to allocate budget for promotion, adding that it would be a futile investment. On the contrary, he claims that it would be sufficient to hook the consumers in the digital world of today!! This is because, according to Eyal, it is very hard for consumers to get out of the hook once they have been hooked. Eyal acknowledges that the hook tactics handled in the book are very effective from the capitalist perspective to engage consumers more at any cost. Eyal has also started to share some strategies that explain how the consumers who have been exposed to an ill-intentioned habit design can get themselves rid of the hook. The TimeWellSpent movement initiated by Google's former ethics executive who had resigned from his position and the Center for Human Technology, among the founders, have gained numerous supporters who maintain that the attention economy needs to be shifted...

The Hook

Figure 7.2: The Hook Model: Source: Nir Eyal

176

> Screen addiction as a devised process is a serious problem that is caused by the use of illusional marketing techniques in an ill-intentioned manner.

Other Side of the Story: Technology Addiction as a Devised Process

Designed Habits

Eyal (2014), who considers habits and power of the variable rewards as the starting point, has added a fourth element into the habit loop that used to have three steps. Thus, he developed the digital product design method that would render experience a habit and therefore cause addiction. Targeting a habit loop that results in addiction, this model, named Hook, is made up of the following steps: trigger (cue), action (routine), reward (variable) and investment (in the platform). The Hook model is explained over the Facebook application as follows: the push notification that comes to the mobile phone from the Facebook application makes up the trigger step. Action is the behavior of entering the mobile application. The variable reward is what the notification is about. For example, the day after the user has uploaded an album with many photos, the user will not be able to see the feedback (variable rewards in this model) on the photograph such as how many people liked which photograph of hers unless she enters the application (doing the action in this model). If one of those who liked the photograph and wrote a comment on it is not among her friends, that person's friend request is defined as the last step of the model, that is to say investment in the platform. The more the investment is, the harder it becomes to quit the platform. In addition, the friendship request causes a new push notification to be sent to the other party. This interactive system keeps its users within a constant loop. It is aimed that in time internal triggers will be more effective than the external ones. An example of an internal trigger would be the loneliness a person might feel or his desire to have more friends.

Other Elements that Cause Addiction on Digital Media

There are several elements which reinforce technology addiction, and these elements are found in digital media, not in other media such as television, books or magazines.

Variable rewards are among the elements that are employed more effectively in digital media compared to other forms of media. Another feature of digital medium is the lack of a stop sign.

Stop Sign: The underlying reason why many activities cause addiction is the mentality of the stop sign. A film that you are watching ends or a book you read has an end too. These are natural stop signs for putting an end to the related activity. Stop sign indicates the end of the activity. Eliminating the stop sign or generating a content presentation that is never ending brings about an increase in consumption. Other than the elements concerning technology handled in this study, studies in different fields also support this finding. Likewise, a study conducted on stop sign, it has been revealed that the soup bowls that are automatically refilled cause 73% more consumption than the regular soup bowls (Wansink, Painter & North, 2005). For this very reason, stop signs have been eliminated in the presentation of technology related services most of the time or the stop sign has been made vague. Social media pages and mobile applications feature infinite scroll.

Unhook Strategies

The preliminary thing to do to neutralize or deactivate the cue, that is the trigger, as the first step of the Hook model, on the smartphones is to turn off all sorts of push notifications from the settings. When it is considered that only 18% of the consumers change the default settings of push notifications, it can be stated that this strategy is simple but effective, and one that is something often disregarded. At this point, the individuals develop the Fear of Missing out (FoMo) or anxiety since they may not be reached when need be due to not seeing the messages or notifications. Ultimately, rather than an order in which technology is the master and the person is the servant, an order in which the person is in charge and in the position of managing things should be taken as a basis. To this end, quality time may be arranged in such a way that meal times and shared activities with family members will be spent with everyone being entirely isolated from technology. If such routines can be rendered habits over time, it will be possible, for certain time intervals, to break the habit of using smart phones unnecessarily, which is triggered by unconscious drives and urges. Besides this, people will be able to discover how enjoyable it is to spend quality time together with others and in a state isolated from technology.

The second step to be employed in order for one to get out of the hook includes making it difficult to take action in a conscious way. The most practical suggestion for this is to eliminate the time-killing social media and texting applications from the mobile phone screens and moving them into the back pages, if possible into sub-folders. Thus, the action stage is rendered difficult and the time it takes to enter the application is made longer. As a result, the system the person finds himself immersed in the technological platform becomes disrupted before the active consciousness comes into play. The other ways of making the action difficult are to enter the application via the internet browser rather than entering into it via the mobile app and log out following each use of it.

In order to get rid of the hook at the reward stage is to delay the reward. For example, while surfing the content website, one may decide to add the articles he wants to read into the reading list of his phone or into an application like 'pocket' (https://getpocket.com/) and to delay the reading activity. In this way, even if one feels the instant urge to do reading, it is possible, in the future, not to read most of the papers procrastinated as a result of adding the articles into the reading list. Another suggestion to prevent the entering into a fast loop is not giving instant responses to WhatsApp messages. When the reverse action is performed, namely if one responds to WhatsApp messages immediately, then an immediate response is written back. Thus, texting turns into the format of chatting and gains continuity accordingly. The same goes for responding to emails. Rather than giving an immediate response to an email message, one may resort to using applications like 'Boomerang' (www.boomerangapp.com) to send the answer in the next day or hour.

References

55. Ertemel, A. V., & Aydın, G. "Technology addiction in the digital economy and suggested solutions," *Addicta: The Turkish Journal on Addictions,* 5 (2018), 665-690.

CONCLUSION

Those days when differentiation of the brands is constrained by the intuition and imagination of the management teams are now over.

The concept of crowdsourcing ensures that consumers can contribute to the brand at all stages with the understanding of prosumers.

—The Marketing Discipline has become more Technical and Measurable than ever.

It has become possible to develop a product by verifying the assumptions related to the customers and products through customer development approach. By means of trying and measuring all possibilities in the business model construction and thus conducting growth hacking, products that can sell themselves can be developed in today's world.

Yet, in the world where marketing has become totally technical through automation, ironically, it is required to resort to emotions and behavioral psychology as well *so as to persuade consumers who have increasingly acquired immunity to the new techniques to engage and interact.*

To this end, it is important to devise a brand story that is based on humanistic values (marketing 3.0) and address the subconscious. Illusional marketing channels people to adopt positive attitudes and display positive behaviors towards the brand by appealing to their subconscious.

As it is the case in the example of the Nike FuelBand of the Nike brand which promises a fitter lifestyle, a sustainable instance of gamification that has a meaningful primary goal for all the 'players' like leading a healthier and fitter life while burning calories to this end could set as a good example of illusional marketing. In contrast, a plot that engages the users in an interaction at the beginning successfully and turns them into addicts would cause the players to leave the game in time and yield an unfavorable outcome for everyone unless it serves a purposeful and meaningful cause.

It is required to perform gamification in line with the philosophy of Marketing 3.0 in a sustainable manner and relating it to people so that they can associate it with themselves rather than implementing gamification through short-term targets and extrinsic motivation. It would be beyond the purpose of playing a game and players will feel that they are a part of a cause and a story which is broader than themselves. When they feel so they can take action in true sense. In the Nike Fuel example, this target is visualized and the users who have the wristband can follow how many times the users are rotating around the world through real time indicators. Thus, the contribution of each user to the story is made evident and the users can feel that too.

In short, the place and significance of stories in our lives will increase every day. And this will, for sure, happen. Similarly, it can be foreseen that the user experience will go through a constant evolution and become perfect in such a way that will enable the consumers to have their interaction with brands, products and services in the smoothest way possible. Yet, the future of gamification, the extent of responsibility it will be handled and the reaction of consumers towards those approaches in the long run will be clearer only in time.

Concluding Remarks ...

The techniques of illusional marketing enable the marketing managers to realize the desired behavior changes, having the inclination to turn them into habits through the use of the unconscious. For this very reason, using the aforementioned weapons in a positive manner would serve humanity. Yet, those very same weapons may also be used in a way that could yield negative consequences like screen addiction as a devised process. In this current era of ours, revealing these techniques starkly along with their positive and negative aspects will be a highly significant task to be fulfilled by academia.

Concluding Remarks

Digital platforms have achieved to "hook" the consumers and make them glued to the screen through the products developed based on the discoveries of the psychologists regarding the way the human brain is working. It is foreseen that these new weapons in the digital toolkit will be even more effective when combined with near future orientations such as augmented reality and virtual reality. Due to the fact that children and youngsters of the Z Generation and its successor Alpha Generation meet digital devices and the internet at an early stage of their lives, the likelihood of such groups to develop addiction to such devices seems rather high.

All in all, the techniques of illusional marketing come to the fore as the new weapons in the toolkit of the brands efficiency of which has been proven. Illusional marketing practices that do not truly serve a meaningful cause may bring about dangerous outcomes. Marketing professionals are to shoulder significant responsibilities at this point. A system that is designed just for the sake of making more money without paying attention to the other dimensions will serve the interest of no party in the long run. Brands will not benefit in the long run either by such a design that disregards the other dimensions.

Adnan Veysel ERTEMEL, PhD.

Istanbul Commerce University

Faculty Member, the Faculty of Business Administration

Adnan Veysel ERTEMEL is Associate Professor of Marketing at İstanbul Ticaret Üniversitesi. He graduated from Yıldız Technical University, Department of Computer Sciences and Engineering in 2000. He received his master's degree in Engineering and Technology Management (ETM) from Boğaziçi University. He started his career as a part time employee in the department of New Business Development at Turkcell in 1998. In 2002, he began work for Telenity Europe as the head of Location-Based Services. In 2003, he was accepted into the Entrepreneur Development Program, the first certified entrepreneurship program in Turkey, at Sabancı University. Upon completing the program, he founded his own company named Persona. During his adventure in entrepreneurship for nine years, he embarked upon innovative mobile projects of various sizes realized in many companies in the GSM sector. Mr. Ertemel received his PhD degree in Marketing from Marmara University in 2010. Since 2011, he has been giving lectures on Digital Marketing, Technology Entrepreneurship, Business Model Innovation and Lean Startup at Bahçeşehir University and afterwards at Istanbul Commerce University. He is also a columnist for publications including HBR Turkey Blog, Fintech Time and Blockchain Time. Besides these, he serves in the management of CDO Turkey, which is an extension of CDO World (Chief Digital Officer), the Union of Chambers and Commodity Exchanges of Turkey and Istanbul Province Board of Young Entrepreneurs.

www.ingramcontent.com/pod-product-compliance
Lightning Source LLC
Chambersburg PA
CBHW031958190326
41520CB00007B/288